THE DARK FOREST ANTHOLOGY OF THE INTERNET

by

THE DARK FOREST COLLECTIVE

Table of contents

7   Foreword
13 Contributors

19 The Dark Forest Theory of the Internet
27 The Extended Internet Universe
41 The Dark Forest and Cozy Web
49 Chapel Perilous
65 We Need New Platforms To Tell New Stories
71 Proof of Vibes
85 Moving Castles
113 The Internet Didn't Kill Counterculture:
    You Just Won't Find It on Instagram
129 The Expanding Dark Forest and Generative AI
141 Holographic Media
167 The Post-Individual

191 Excerpt: The Dark Forest
193 Glossary

Yancey Strickler
Venkatesh Rao
Maggie Appleton
Peter Limberg and Rebecca Fox
Joshua Citarella
Leïth Benkhedda
Arthur Röing Baer & GVN908
Caroline Busta

Maggie Appleton
Caroline Busta & Lil Internet
Yancey Strickler

Cixin Liu

The Dark Forest Theory of the Internet

Foreword

This book is about how to survive on the internet.
 Not individual human survival. The survival of ideas.
 The survival of ways of life. The survival of different.
 This book collects essays written by eleven authors asynchronously without coordination over the course of five years. The eleven of us are spread around the world— Berlin, London, New York, Seattle, Toronto. We have very different personal and professional backgrounds. But online we are more alike than different. We're all members and leaders of online communities (including New Models, Do Not Research, Trust, Ribbonfarm, The Stoa, and Metalabel) that exemplify new forms of social institutions that have become increasingly important as the digital world has matured.
 The Anthology started unknowingly in 2017 when one of us, Yancey Strickler, wrote a piece titled "The Dark Forest Theory of the Internet" that connected the author's struggle to be themselves online with an increasing sense of threat and danger on the internet. The essay used the metaphor of the "Dark Forest"— introduced in Fermi's Paradox and written about by the Chinese sci-fi author Cixin Liu in his Three Body Problem trilogy—to bridge those feelings.
 Bringing these ideas together—an increasing reluctance to be real online, a growing need for digital safety, and

the metaphor of the Dark Forest—helped articulate a personal truth that quickly spread. The essay was initially sent to a private newsletter list of 500 people, but as happens with ideas on the internet, was widely shared and soon read by hundreds of thousands of people. As the essay spread, other writers began to engage with and build on its feelings and ideas.

Within days of that first essay, the prolific writer and thinker Venkatesh Rao wrote a prescient follow-up in his Ribbonfarm newsletter that explored the Dark Forest from new angles, introducing the concept of the "CozyWeb" to describe a more homesteading-like experience that defined a certain strata of behavior online.

A few days later, the developer and designer Maggie Appleton brought the Dark Forest and CozyWeb concepts together into a striking illustration that told a new story about the internet as not one place, but a whole topography comprised of multiple levels of safety and security. These three pieces are collected in the first section of this anthology.

In the years following, these ideas continued to travel and connect as the number of Dark Forest spaces grew. When COVID hit, these spaces went from the Very Online digital fringe to a mainstream experience at an unimaginably mass scale.

The second section of the Anthology, titled "Into the Dark Forest," captures that transition with four pieces reflecting the increased importance of digital spaces during the COVID era.

"Chapel Perilous" by Peter Limberg and Rebecca Fox of the stoic community The Stoa combines a mysterious narrative and hand-inked drawings to capture the emotional experience of the descent into our new social reality.

"We Need New Platforms to Tell New Stories" by artist Joshua Citerella narrates the author's decision to leave the confines of academia for a more Dark Forest-based existence.

"Proof of Vibes" by Leïth Benkhedda documents the transition of online life before and after COVID, tracking the author's deepening relationship with online communities and the changes they provoked in his and our personal and collective psychologies.

"Moving Castles" by Arthur Röing Baer and GVN908 of the Berlin-based Trust translates the Dark Forest concept into a forward-looking, modular strategy for communities to balance their own private ways of being while influencing the world beyond their walled garden.

Post-COVID, the need for Dark Forests to help us live and express ourselves online did not go away. As platforms stumbled from short-sighted, trust-destroying decisions, the online landscape arguably saw more upheaval than the physical world. Aspirations of truth, community, membership, and belonging remained, but our existing playbooks and ways of thinking felt increasingly out of step in a new landscape.

The early days of this period are explored in four essays in the Anthology's final section, called "The Dark Forest Era."

In "The internet didn't kill counterculture—you just won't find it on Instagram" (originally published in Document), the cultural critic and writer Caroline Busta of the popular New Models podcast digs into how culture travels and is preserved in an era of Clear Nets—the open web—and Dark Forests — the private spaces where people feel safe to explore and create subcultures together.

In "The Expanding Dark Forest and Generative AI," Maggie Appleton returns to imagine the potential status quo of the post-human internet.

"Holographic Media," a second piece by Caroline Busta and her New Models cohost Lil Internet, connects the weird tendrils and expressions of an increasingly atomized online cultural experience, analyzing the motivations behind them and projecting what the future(s) of media might look like.

In the final piece, "The Post-Individual," published for

the first time here, Yancey Strickler connects our individual and collective experiences to a bigger series of changes stretching from the birth of Christianity to the invention of the individual to the introduction of the computer to many steps yet to come.

The overall arc of these pieces—all written over a span of five very tumultuous years online—illustrates a key evolutionary moment in the social life of the internet. This was the moment the web's youthful exuberance and naiveté gave way to anxiety, self-protection, and a thirst for social structures that could provide safety, meaning, and context in a newly adversarial realm.

We as eleven loosely connected individuals came together to make this collection to reflect this transitory moment. To leave graffiti on humanity's bathroom wall to say here's what it was like to be alive then. Here's what we felt. Here's what we were afraid of. Here's how we tried to collectively and individually self-manage a social revolution churning all around us.

We cannot say where this is going. We can only say where we've been. Welcome to the Dark Forest Anthology of the Internet.

Yancey Strickler, Venkatesh Rao, Maggie Appleton,
Peter Limberg, Rebecca Fox,
Leïth Benkhedda, Joshua Citarella, Arthur Röing Baer,
GVN908, Caroline Busta, Julian Wadsworth

December, 2023, Earth

Contributors
or The Dark Forest Collective

1. Maggie Appleton

Maggie Appleton sits at the intersection of design, anthropology, and programming. Currently a Product Designer at Ought, her work fits under the umbrellas of UX design, visual interface design, and DX. Maggie creates illustrated essays and visual explanations about programming and culture, and advocates for Digital Gardening, tools for thought, and end-user programming.

2. Arthur Röing Baer

Arthur Röing Baer is a designer and organizer. He is a co-founder of Trust, a project space in Berlin for utopian conspiracy and platform design, and co-founder of Moving Castles, a game studio and design lab for autonomous worlds.

3. Leïth Benkhedda

Leïth Benkhedda is a designer, researcher, service provider, and information age hunter-gatherer. His practice explores concepts of autonomy, cooperation, ownership, and governance, both on and off-line. He is a founding member of the Berlin based collective Black Swan, 1/4 of New Models, and one of Trust's co-maintainers. Leïth holds a bachelor's degree in design from the Royal Academy of Arts in The Hague and completed his MFA at the Sandberg Institute.

4. Caroline Busta

Caroline Busta is a Berlin-based writer/consultant and co-founder of New Models (https://newmodels.io), a media platform and community addressing the emergent effects of networked technology on art, tech, politics, and pop-culture. Previously Editor-in-Chief of Texte zur Kunst (2014-17) and an Assoc. Editor of Artforum (2008-14), she is a founding member of the web3 media protocol Channel.xyz.

5. Joshua Citarella

Joshua Citarella is an artist and internet culture researcher. He studied at the School of Visual Arts, New York City. He has been a professor at the School of Visual Arts (2018-19) and the Rhode Island School of Design (2020). Citarella is the author of Politigram & the Post-left (2018) and 20 Interviews (2020). He is the founder of Do Not Research (2021).

6. Rebecca Fox

Rebecca Fox is a ritualist, artist, and writer living in the south of England with her husband and cat. Find out more at rebeccafox.substack.com/about

7. GVN908

GVN908 is a designer with a background in cinema and procedural storytelling. Alumni of Fabrica, the Jan Van Eyck Academie, the Sandberg Instituut, and lecturer on real-time CG at Goldsmiths University, London and Staedelschule, Frankfurt.

8. Lil internet

Lil Internet is a full-stack creative director and a co-founder of New Models (https://newmodels.io). Based in Berlin since 2015, he's directed music videos for Beyoncé, Diplo, and Iggy Azalea; produced tracks for Azealia Banks; and his writing has been published by outlets such as Artforum, Dazed, Texte zur Kunst, Kaleidoscope, and 032c. He is also a founding member of the web3 media protocol Channel.xyz.

9. Peter Limberg

Peter Limberg stewards an in-person and online community called The Stoa.

Residing in Toronto, Canada, he currently writes for the Less Foolish Substack.

10. Venkatesh Rao
Venkatesh Rao is a writer and consultant. He writes the Ribbonfarm blog, and is the author of Tempo, a book on decision-making. He holds a PhD in Aerospace Engineering (2003) from the University of Michigan. He is currently based in Seattle.

11. Yancey Strickler
Yancey Strickler is a writer and entrepreneur. He's the cofounder of Metalabel, cofounder of Kickstarter, and cofounder of the artist resource The Creative Independent. He's the author of This Could Be Our Future: A Manifesto for a More Generous World, the philosophy of Bentoism, and he created the record label eMusic Selects. Yancey began his career as a music critic writing for Pitchfork, Spin, and The Village Voice. He grew up on a farm in Clover Hollow, Virginia, and lives in New York City.

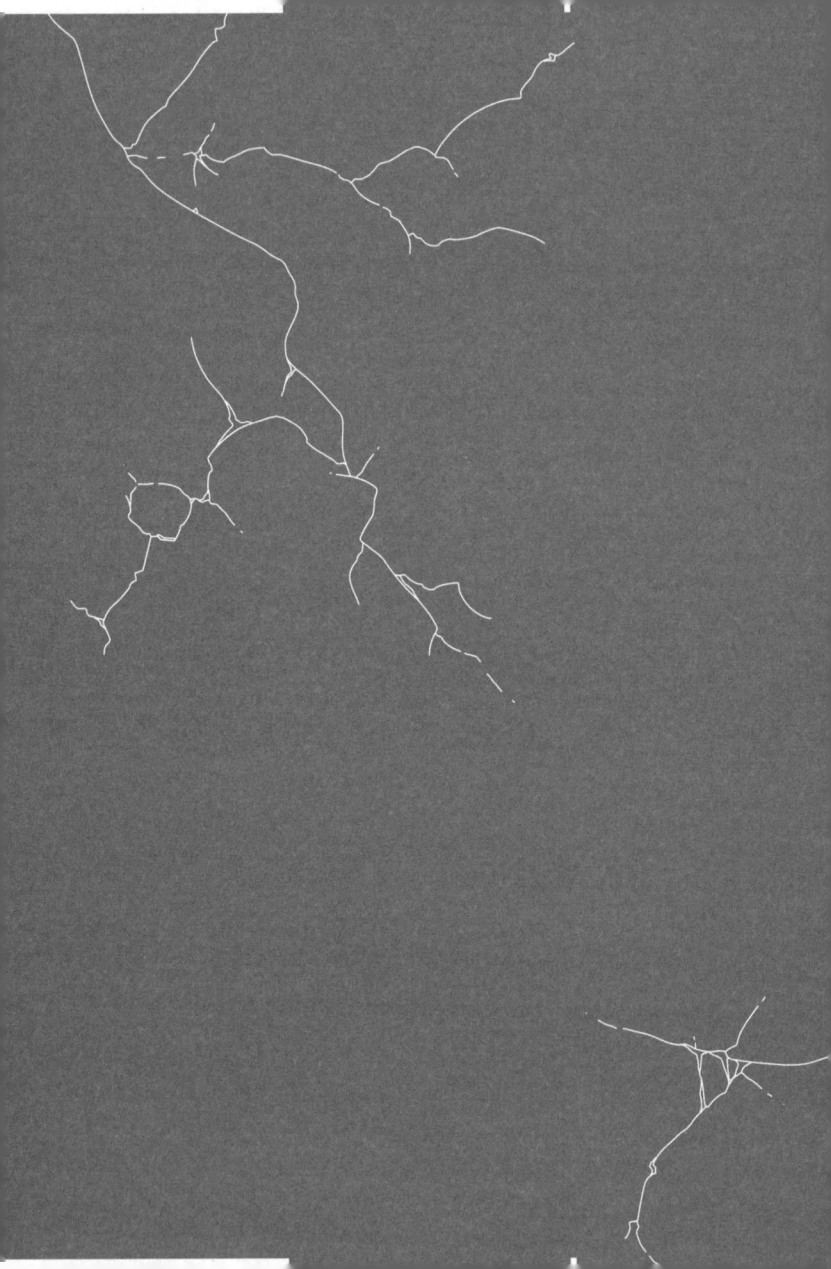

DISCOVERING THE DARK FOREST

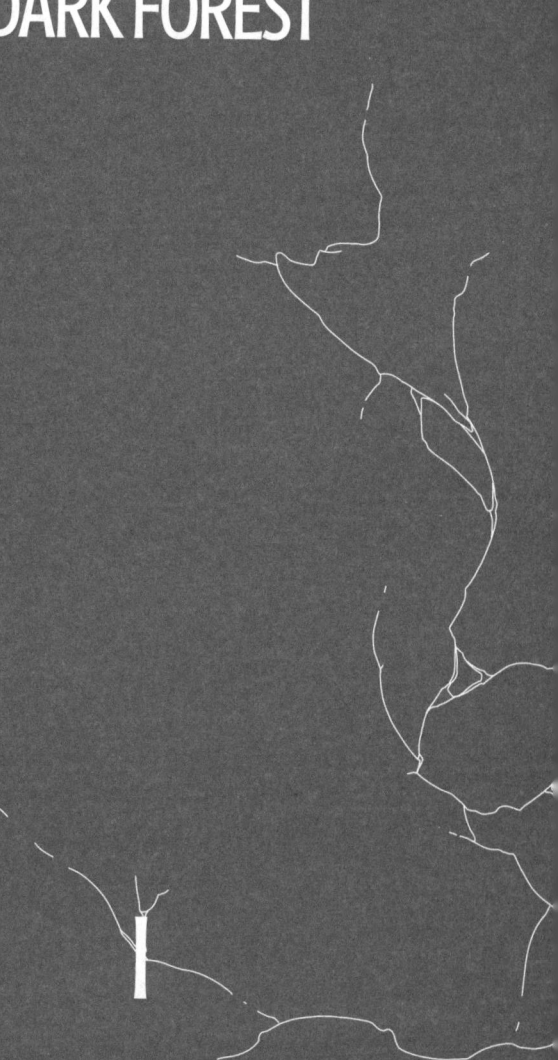

16.05.2019

The Dark Forest Theory of The Internet
by Yancey Strickler

In his sci-fi trilogy The Three Body Problem, author Liu Cixin presents the dark forest theory of the universe.

When we look out into space, the theory goes, we're struck by its silence. It seems like we're the only ones here. After all, if other forms of life existed, wouldn't they show themselves? Since they haven't, we assume there's no one else out there.

Liu invites us to think about this a different way.

Imagine a dark forest at night. It's deathly quiet. Nothing moves. Nothing stirs. This could lead one to assume that the forest is devoid of life. But it's not. The dark forest is full of life. It's quiet because night is when the predators come out. To survive, the animals stay quiet.

Is our universe an empty forest or a dark one? If it's a dark forest, then only Earth is foolish enough to ping the heavens and announce its presence. The rest of the universe already knows the real reason why the forest stays dark. It's only a matter of time before the Earth learns as well.

This is also what the internet is becoming: a dark forest.

In response to the ads, the tracking, the trolling, the hype, and other predatory behaviors, we're retreating to our dark forests of the internet, and away from the mainstream.

This very email is an example of this. This theory is

being shared on a private channel sent to 500 people who I know or who have explicitly chosen to receive it. This is the online environment in which I feel most secure. Where I can be my most "real self."

Podcasts are another example. There, meaning isn't just expressed through language, but also through intonation and interaction. Podcasts are where a bad joke can still be followed by a self-aware and self-deprecating save. Like newsletters, what's said in podcasts is non-indexed, non-optimized, and non-gamified. It's a more forgiving space for communication than the internet at large.

Dark forests like newsletters and podcasts are growing areas of activity. As are other dark forests, like Slack channels, private Instagrams, invite-only message boards, text groups, Snapchat, WeChat, and on and on.

These are all spaces where depressurized conversation is possible because of their non-indexed, non-optimized, and non-gamified environments. The cultures of those spaces have more in common with the physical world than the internet.

The internet of today is a battleground. The idealism of the '90s web is gone. The Web 2.0 utopia—where we all lived in rounded filter bubbles of happiness—ended with the 2016 Presidential election when we learned that the tools we thought were only life-giving could be weaponized as well. The public and semi-public spaces we created to develop our identities, cultivate communities, and gain in knowledge were overtaken by forces using them to gain power of various kinds (market, political, social, and so on).

This is the atmosphere of the mainstream web today: a relentless competition for power. As this competition has grown in size and ferocity, an increasing number of the population has scurried into their dark forests to avoid the fray.

The Web 2.0 era has been replaced by a new Web^2 era. An age where we simultaneously live in many different internets whose numbers increase hourly. The dark forests are growing.

The dark forests grow because they provide psychological and reputational cover. They allow us to be ourselves because we know who else is there. Compared to the free market communication style of the mass channels—with their high risks, high rewards, and limited moderation—dark forest spaces are more Scandinavian in their values and the social and emotional security they provide. They cap the downsides of looking bad and the upsides of our best jokes by virtue of a contained audience.

This is a trade more and more people are looking to make.

⅓ The Bowling Alley Theory of the Internet

I went dark on the internet a few years ago. I took social apps off my phone, unfollowed everyone, the whole shebang. This was without a doubt a good decision. I've been happier and have had better control over my time since. Many others have done this and are doing this. A generation of modern wannabe monks.

But even as my personal wellness grows, I see a risk in this change.

You could argue that these decisions removed me from the arena. I detached from the mainstream of conversation. I stopped watching TV. I stopped looking at Facebook and Twitter. I silenced my voice on the platforms where conversation was happening because of the strings, risks, and side effects they created in return.

This detachment wasn't just in politics. It was also true of how I shared my personal life. Milestones for me and my family were left unshared beyond our internet dark forests, even though many more friends and members of our families would've been happy to hear about them.

Not sharing was my choice, of course, and I didn't

The dark forests grow because they provide psychological and reputational cover

They allow us to be ourselves because we know who else is there

question it. My alienation from the mainstream was their loss, not mine. But did this choice also deprive me of some greater reward?

Not everyone who joined a bowling league (when people did such things) loved bowling. Many loved being with other people first and bowling came second or not at all. Being together is what mattered. The venue did not.

This is the Bowling Alley Theory of the Internet: that people are online purely to meet each other, and in the long run the venues where we congregate are an unimportant background compared to the interactions themselves. Did we meet on MySpace, Tinder, or LinkedIn? Does it matter?

When I went offline for reasons of personal wellness and productivity, I stopped going to the bowling alleys altogether. But lately I've started to question that decision.

I'm reminded of what happened in the 1970s when the hippies—bruised and bloodied from the culture wars of the '60s—retreated into self-help, wellness, and personal development, as Adam Curtis documents in his series The Century of Self. While they turned inward, the winners of the '60s culture wars took society's reigns. A focus on personal wellness created an unintended side effect: a retreat from the public arena, and a shift in the distribution of power ever since.

It's possible, I suppose, that a shift away from the mainstream internet and into the dark forests could permanently limit the mainstream's influence. It could de-legitimize it. In some ways that's the story of the internet's effect on broadcast television. But we forget how powerful television still is. And those of us building dark forests risk underestimating how powerful the mainstream channels will continue to be, and how minor our havens are compared to their immensity.

The influence of Facebook, Twitter, and others is enormous and not going away. There's a reason why Russian military focused on these platforms when they wanted to manipulate public opinion: they have real impact. The meaning and tone of these platforms changes with who uses them. What kind of bowling alley it is depends on who goes there.

Should a significant percentage of the population abandon these spaces, that will leave nearly as many eyeballs for those who are left to influence, and limit the influence of those who departed on the larger world they still live in.

If the dark forest isn't dangerous already, these departures might ensure that it will be.

24.05.2019

The Extended Internet Universe
by Venkatesh Rao

For several years now, I've been watching the creeping, unheralded growth of what I call the cozyweb, and for which others have lots of creative names. Kickstarter founder Yancey Strickler called it the Dark Forest in a recent post.

Unlike the main public internet, which runs on the (human) protocol of "users" clicking on links on public pages/apps maintained by "publishers," the cozyweb works on the (human) protocol of everybody cutting-and-pasting bits of text, images, URLs, and screenshots across live streams. Much of this content is poorly addressable, poorly searchable, and very vulnerable to bitrot. It lives in a high-gatekeeping slum-like space comprising slacks, messaging apps, private groups, storage services like Dropbox, and of course, email.

Public and cozy are just two of the dozens of distinctly different flavors of internet around today. Here's my attempt at mapping the complexity of the extended internet universe.

Think of it as a vertical section through the nominal internet (everything connected via TCP/IP). The vertical dimension is depth and complexity of the permission/security architecture you need to navigate to access things. The horizontal dimension goes from darkweb with little to no public internet activity to the well-lit web, with lots of

Unplugged Darkness

both public and private activity.

So there's this 2x2 under the hood here, with high to low risk on the x-axis and high to low privacy on the y-axis. The x-axis itself is the private-to-public boundary, marked by email for most of us. The y-axis is the high-risk to low-risk boundary, marked by security stronger/weaker than simple passwords for most of us.

1/5 Top Left

As you might expect, the high-risk, low-privacy quadrant is mostly empty (except for accidental or malicious disclosures like leaked information). The "Darkness" above the "Dark Web" is missing publicly visible activity. Activity might appear there in collapsed societies with no state power, where underworld elements can brazenly wander about in the light of day, OR in highly open utopian societies where there are no taboos, people leave their doors open, and there is no use for locks. The top left quadrant is basically empty/dark because both pure utopias and dystopias are hard to sustain for longer than five minutes.

2/5 Top Right

Darkness is the natural dual of the adtech web, the zone of extreme overactivity above the surface of the cozyweb, with businesses trying desperately to penetrate into private spaces past the open-to-private boundary marked by email. This makes poetic sense. The adtech world is neither utopian nor dystopian. It is pragmatically mehtopian. It's the essence of the mediocre world we have, whatever the world we want might look like.

One reason I'm jumping on the substack bandwagon with two of my newsletters is that it is an interesting bet against the ad-supported public internet. CEO Chris Best argues that podcasts need to go from ad-supported to

The cozyweb retreats from public view for various reasons ranging from simple

The Dark Forest Theory of the Internet

preference for privacy and small communities to fear and PTSD

subscription-based. This idea wouldn't have been possible as recently as ten years ago due to the jankiness of payments infrastructure.

The argument generalizes beyond podcasts. Increasingly, the only reasons to do "free" content at significant scale are bad ones, involving manipulation of crowd sentiments. The ad-based internet isn't the cause of that, but it certainly makes it indefinitely sustainable.

3/5 Center and Top

The center and top of the map/2x2 form a sort of Yggdrasil public world tree through which the long-distance spooky entanglements of the extended internet operate.

The core of the internet is still the public web (which on the 2x2 sprawls across all 4 quadrants rather untidily), and though the rest of the world may not like the idea, it's still primarily US-centric. To the extent other nations have created distinct internet flavors, they exist as restricted publics on top of the US-centric global public web. I've shown this as the purplish upper branches.

Between those branches we find old media — gray ladies in their gray gardens? Which is an authoritarian information space by the standards of the modern extended internet universe. I think it makes poetic sense to classify things like newspapers and cable television channels with (say) the Chinese and other less-free-than-American internets. The level of regulation and top-down control of information flows is comparable.

The American internet may head in that direction as well in the future, leaving an entire dark middle band: 2/3 dark (modulo leaks), 1/3 ads (aside: ads are "darkness" content too in a sense, since we all try our best not to look at them).

4/5 Bottom

The dotted lines connecting the archipelagos in the bottom half of the map are cut-and-paste type human protocol activity, often even air-gapped human transfers (business cards, scribbled email addresses, all the way to secret single-use darkweb addresses passed on through dead drops).

In the lower right cozyweb archipelago, this is just permissions negotiated via meatspace handshakes with no particularly serious security concerns. Most of the >1:1 cozyweb spaces I'm part of have an informal FrieNDA (friendly NDA) in effect, but much of it is merely boringly private. Pajama web rather than cloak-and-dagger web.

I'm brewing cloak-and-dagger conspiracies only in a few select channels. Like most sane people, if I actually wanted to do dark and devious stuff, I'd keep it all entirely offline and conduct my dirty business in close-up whispers with the shower on, music blaring, and wearing a tinfoil hat. Even supposedly "encrypted" apps (modulo NSA backdoors) are risky if you actually want to pick a significant fight with a powerful adversary.

That's the zone on the lower left, where there are security concerns and hostile intentions all around, and lots of associated technology like VPNs, stronger-than-passwords security models, etc. In that corner, the corporate deep web morphs into the government-corporate deep-state web of security and law-enforcement agencies, whitehat/blackhat hackers, and then into the dark web proper, of drugs, assassination contracts, and child porn.

But the big story is the perfectly legal cozyweb. More and more civilian online activity is sinking into the cozyweb. It doesn't have a good interconnection fabric (ie, it's all about the sophistication of cut-and-paste). It has better boundary/gatekeeping technology (administration, kicking users out) than linking technology. The cut-and-paste-and-screenshot protocol could use some good, deeper productization.

Apparently, Japan has already been down this road (ht Adam Elkus) with people retreating from the public internet to the cozy internet.

The cozynet is not the same as waldenponding, since it remains connected and online and isn't concerned about distraction or overuse of digital media. It just retreats from public view/activity for various reasons ranging from simple preference for privacy and small communities to fear and PTSD.

5/5 The Pick-2-of-3

The current governing logic of the extended internet universe, I think, boils down to a pick-2-of-3 constraint triangle: free, open to the public, quality.

Can we have all three? Many idealists think we once had that (we never did, we just had small scale, and it still wasn't hitting all three), or that in some hand-wavy way, "true" net neutrality would deliver that (I'm only a very weak defender of net neutrality: it was a useful principle for a while, but it has outlived its utility).

I think we can get closer than we are today though.

That's the promise of the crypto world (not just cryptocurrencies, but cryptographic technologies in general, starting with private-key based identity and security for everything). It is still at a very rudimentary stage of development. But once it matures, we will see the entire extended internet universe getting rearchitected on better foundations where we could at least push out the boundary of the 2-of-3 pareto.

For example, the cozyweb could evolve from cut-and-paste to a personal blockchain of context-permissioned, addressable, searchable, interlinked clips. Disqus comes architecturally close with its commenting system, but requires publishers to cooperate, with no meaningful incentives to do so. Plus it is public rather than private, and relies

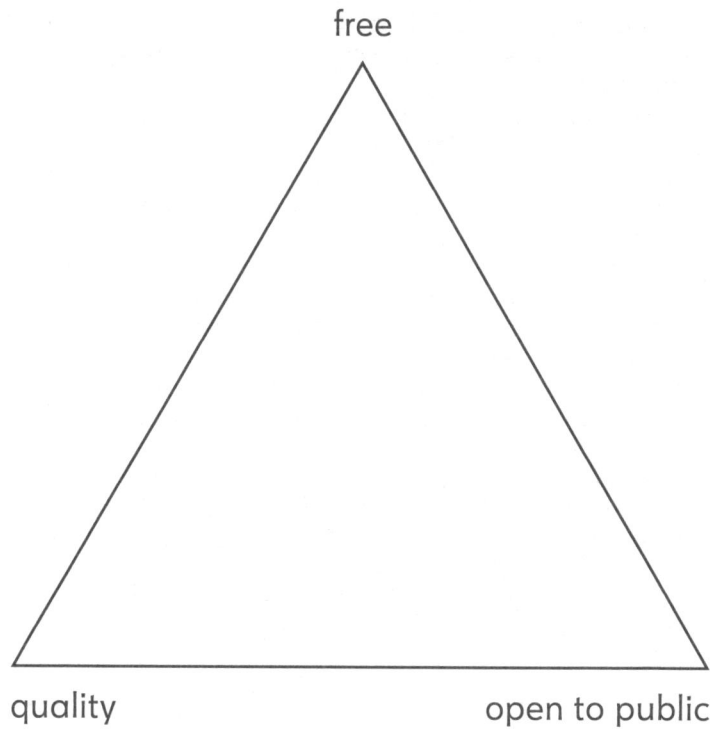

on a trusted 3rd party, and the idea that trusted 3rd parties are security holes is one of the doctrinal foundations of all things crypto.

Disqus is also simply too old technologically, since it dates to an era when "commenting" was a thing. The cozyweb may have been born as the comments section of the public internet forking off, but is now a vastly bigger, more complex space.

This observation generalizes: a LOT of the problems of the internet are due to much of it being simply too old. It wasn't built to last this long even conceptually (i.e. in terms of atomic ideas like "comments"), let alone technologically. We need improvements, upgrades, and modernizations. The industrial world did that, and the internet world will have to as well.

Things were so simple 20 or even 10 years ago (social media, dated to the invention of RSS, is 20 years old, bitcoin is 10 years old). In 1999, there was the Internet, and there were various Intranets.

Then things got complicated. There are interesting times ahead.

28.05.2019

The Dark Forest and the Cozy Web
by Maggie Appleton

The cozy web is Venkatesh Rao's term for the private, gatekeeper-bounded spaces of the internet we have all retreated to over the last few years.

It's the "high-gatekeeping slum-like space comprising slacks, messaging apps, private groups, storage services like dropbox, and of course, email." The informal, untracked, messily human space that the bots and algorithms haven't infiltrated yet.

Venkat first proposed the term in one of his Breaking Smart emails on The Extended Internet Universe. He builds off Yancey Strickler's companion idea of the Dark Forest theory of the web. The "dark forest" is a place that seems eerily quiet and devoid of life. All the living creatures within it are hiding. Because "night is when the predators come out. To survive, the animals stay silent."

The predators here are the advertisers, tracking bots, clickbait creators, attention-hungry influencers, reply guys, and trolls. It's unsafe to reveal yourself to them in any authentic way. So we retreat into private spaces. We hide in the cozy web.

Loving both of these notions, I felt compelled to bring them together into an illustrated diagram of our current social internet situation.

> "These are all spaces where depressurized conversation is possible because of their non-indexed, non-optimized, and non-gamified environments"

Yancey Strickler – The Dark Forest Theory of the Internet

We create tiny underground burrows of Slack channels, Whatsapp groups, Discord chats, and Telegram streams that offer shelter and respite from the aggressively public nature of Facebook, Twitter, and every recruiter looking to connect on LinkedIn.

It's the digital realm of Domestic Cozy Gen-Z vibes. Casual, comfy, and not trying to kick up a fuss.

The cozy web works on "(human) protocol of everybody cutting-and-pasting bits of text, images, URLs, and screenshots across live streams", hopefully one day evolving "from cut-and-paste to a personal blockchain of context-permissioned, addressable, searchable, interlinked clips" as Venkat puts it.

It's since become a standard part of the Venkat Vocabulary for fellow Ribbonfarmers and Yaks, and remains one of my favourite Neologisms of this year.

We create tiny underground burrows that offer shelter and respite

The Dark Forest Theory of the Internet

from the aggressively public nature of Facebook and Twitter

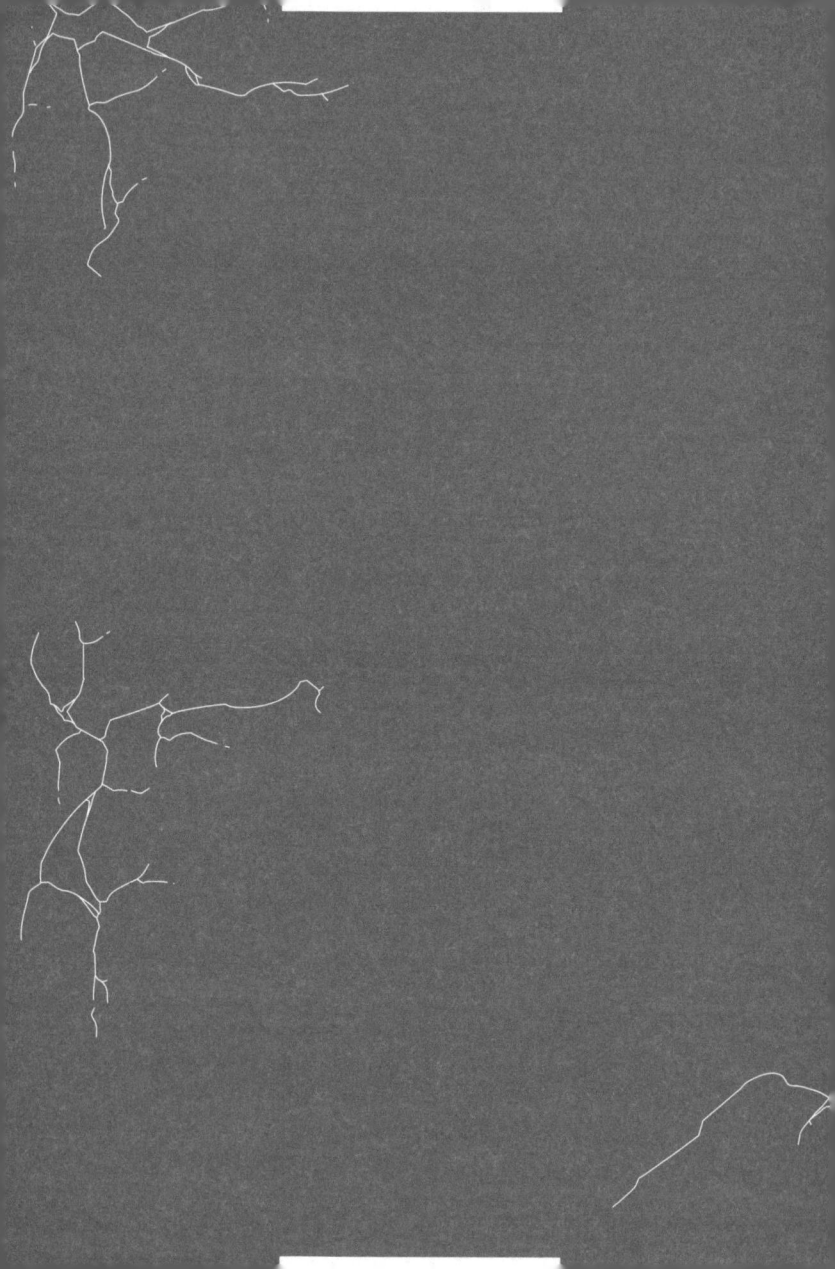

INTO THE DARK FOREST

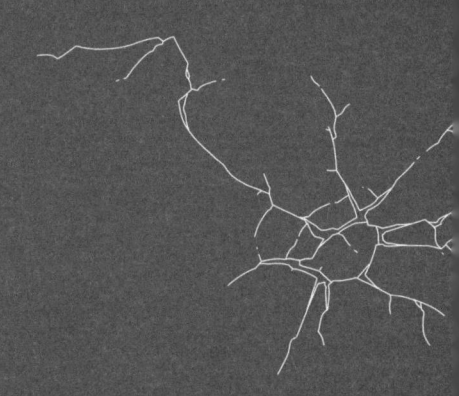

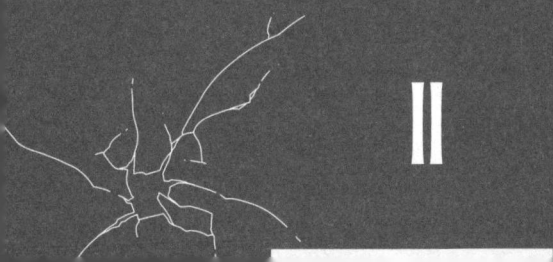

II

27.02.2021

Chapel Perilous
by Peter Limberg and Rebecca Fox

¼ The Edge

You finally found the others. You were so sure of it. They believed what you believed, got outraged by what outraged you, and had the same aesthetic tastes as you, not to mention the same enemies. It felt nourishing, therapeutic, even tribal.

Memes—in the colloquial sense of the word—were being circulated within your tribe, liked and shared again and again, reaffirming your shared beliefs. These captioned images seemed cute and harmless enough, but another type of meme was being shared alongside them: "units of cultural transmission," as Richard Dawkins phrased it.

Memes have the power to captivate an entire group of people. In the internet age, these groups are referred to as "memetic tribes," and there are many of them. Some coexist peacefully, others not so much. These tribes have a meme complex, or memeplex, which can enthrall a group by offering its members what they most desire: a sense of belonging.

Who are these memetic tribes? Some are from the left or right of the political spectrum, others claim the center, or float up to the meta. The more vocal ones currently are issue based, focusing on gender, race, and other causes surrounding social justice. Some are not political at all, and are tribal around spiritual or religious lines, concerned with things like justifying God's existence or attempting to undermine the justification of God's existence.

All tribes speak to each other in a language of memes. From the safe distance of the internet, these shared languages provide a sense of connection and affirmation that makes us feel understood. And more importantly, they make us feel right.

But these emotions are fleeting. Boredom creeps in as belonging fades. Genuinely questioning the contours of your tribe's meme space will get you in trouble. You will be labeled as foolish, a "concern troll," or worse, a traitor. You soon learn there is no room for dissent, and you begin to intimately understand the boundaries of your tribe.

You find yourself pushed to the margins. From there you can see the edges of memetic foreign lands. Other exiles stand at those edges, questioning their tribes' meme space. The content of their questions is quite different, but you sense the spirit of their questioning is the same.

2/4 The Descent

You found your tribe because you were a seeker, because you cared about the truth, and for a while your truth-hunger was satiated. You felt like you had finally arrived. But now things are different.

You feel alienated. You realize there is no room for exploration within your tribe, and exploration is what you need; the cracks are showing, and you cannot ignore them any longer. Enough is enough. The mystery calls, and you begin to descend. You know there are others out there, you saw them at the edge, and heard the murmurs of their questioning, which seemed so similar to your own.

You're on your own now. Tribeless, once again.

The certainty you once had is now gone, along with the memes that helped you feel at home. Uncertainty is overcoming you. You judge yourself: you are too old for this shit. You should know who you are by now, you should know how to live your life by now. You've missed your chapel of knowingness, and you long for a map of reality, one that shows you the territory, once and for all.

If you asked a psychologist they'd tell you that you're experiencing an "Intolerance of Uncertainty." It's only human, and the symptoms are all there: rumination, restlessness, anxiety, and, of course, existential loneliness, the kind that has been following you around your whole life. There is no turning back now with all this unknowingness, that much you know. The way through is to keep going. You see the darkness ahead.

¾ The Forest

"Great doubt, great awakening. Little doubt, little awakening. No doubt, fast asleep."

You do not know what is true anymore, but this Zen maxim seems true enough. You have fully descended into a dark forest, surrounded by the unknown. A great doubt has seeped in, and questions start rushing in your mind at a maddening pace ...

Will I always feel this lost?
Will I always feel this crazy?
Will I always feel this alone?

The last one stings the most. You are surprised by this. Maybe this is not about retiring past truths to simply replace them with new ones. Maybe this great doubt is not about finding the truth at all...

You realize you were sleepwalking through life before this, and more tragically, you were not really seeing people as the mystery that they are. You were filtering them through the lens of your retired truths.

In the thick of the unknown, you are afraid: afraid of who you were, and of who you may become, but with this fear there is a sense of aliveness. You hear something. It sounds familiar, and matches the murmurs you heard before in the distance.

Another approaches. The person you saw at the edge. You feel their fear. You also feel their sense of aliveness. Starting conversations with strangers in dark forests does not seem advisable, but maybe Timothy Leary was right when he advised the following ...

Who knows what you might learn from taking a chance on conversation with a stranger? Everyone carries a piece of the puzzle. Nobody comes into your life by mere coincidence. Trust your instincts. Do the unexpected. Find the others...

Finding the others. Maybe this is what a great doubt was really for.

4/4 The Chapel

Your new friend is different in many ways. They tell you about the memetic tribe they were once memeing with. It is different from yours. You do not fully get it, and you are surprised by how cool you are with not getting it.

You notice that you do not have a sense of judgment towards them, like you would have had before. You notice that they are not judging you as well. Something else is similar: they are going through a great doubt too, experiencing the same confusion, fear, and aliveness that you are experiencing.

A purple light appears, and you see a neon sign flickering. The sign reads "Chapel Perilous," and the purple light starts to reveal the contours of a structure, one that does not seem to belong to this time. It seems like it does not belong to time at all.

This chapel has an inviting quality. Your new friend says

they feel it as well. You both are compelled to go inside. You move towards it to get a closer look, and when you do, your sense of fear starts to dissipate. The confusion you felt is still here, but you no longer view it as a negative thing. A desire to celebrate the confusion starts to bubble up.

Others emerge from the dark forest; exiles from other memetic tribes, longing to find the others. You feel more you, in an embodied way. You do not have the desire to understand yourself in the way your memetic tribe understood you, and you already feel more understood by how this emerging embodied tribe does not understand you.

You stay with the paradox. You embrace the mystery. You enter the chapel.

Will I always feel this lost?
Will I always feel this crazy?
Will I always feel this alone?

The Dark Forest Theory of the Internet

Will I always feel this lost?
Will I always feel this crazy?
Will I always feel this alone?

20.09.2021

We Need New Platforms To Tell New Stories
by Joshua Citarella

This September, I'm not going back to teaching. I've spent the past few years arguing against the idea that online platforms could be a suitable replacement for institutions. But now, I'm leaving my university jobs to become a content creator.

As the US went into lockdown and all of higher education rapidly transitioned into Zoom meetings, a Twitch stream and a college classroom suddenly felt very similar. In August of 2020, I uploaded my syllabus to the crowdfunding platform Patreon. Within a few months, a group of extremely active and dedicated art students had collected in the community Discord server. They formed a reading group and taught the syllabus material to themselves.

Most members of this online community are recent graduates of BFA programs. Some are older and some are younger. Some have graduate degrees and others never went to art school. All of them use this space as a supplement, or replacement, for their accredited education. It's the same syllabus that I used to teach at prestigious schools, but these new students are more engaged and we can speak more honestly about art, politics, and everything else.

Perhaps the biggest question is why I had to resort to crowdfunding in the first place. A few years ago, when social media, online aesthetics, and radical politics reshaped the national discourse, the "aesthetic experts" of the art world had seemingly nothing to say about it. For all the many volumes of texts and hours of documentaries produced on these topics, it seems awfully strange that there are no paintings to go along with it. I can count on a single hand the number of professional artists who made work dealing with these subjects.

I've spent the last few years researching young online memetic subcultures that have now grown into radical movements and are effecting real political shifts offline. Art that engages with relevant and discursively significant topics usually attracts some level of collector interest. Or, when the market fails to support this work, there are grants and other institutional flows that step in to facilitate such projects. But as online aesthetics became more relevant than ever, there were simply no resources mobilized and no work made to address these urgent topics. When you do not see the world reflected in art, you know that something is deeply wrong.

Soon, we arrive at the meta-problem: today's unprecedented polarization of wealth, that which feeds private collections and institutional funding, is the cause of radical politics. Within the professional art world, it is simply not possible to make work about these subjects, because the donor class will not facilitate critiques of their real power. In hindsight, it seems obvious.

Situating my research at the edge of the art world attracted a community of creative people, many of whom were also interested to address these important topics in their own projects. So we gathered it all together and published it. DoNotResearch.net is a platform for essays, visual art, video, poetry, music, and internet culture research. The community organizes reading groups, community workshops, lectures and more. In the absence of a place to explore counter-narratives and investigate what we took to be the pressing topics of the present, we built our own space online.

A crowdfunded creative think-tank can churn out opinion pieces without fear of reprisal or worry that its funding might be cut. Its independence is what makes it valuable. We are proving that these topics are indeed relevant and that they warrant discussion by aesthetic experts. We will become the institution that we know is missing.

Through my writing, podcasts and streams, I've tried to relay a simple provocation for young artists: this education and career path is training you to become part of a professional class that, in reality, no longer exists. Institutions pay below market rates and no longer offer the protections that allowed artists to engage with complex ideas.
Right now, you're at a crossroads where you can choose to either hold the line for elite interests that refuse to facilitate the work you know is important, or you can leave and make whatever you want.

We will become the institution

The Dark Forest Theory of the Internet

that we know is missing

10.07.2021

The Dark Forest Theory of the Internet

Proof of Vibes
by Leïth Benkhedda

As "Stay home" became the new "Go outside" in the early days of the year 2020, the Internet replaced the classroom, the bar, the cinema, the library, the office, and other IRL spaces I used to inhabit. The "new normal" some would say as others begged them to shut up. Some could afford to log-off, relocate to their countryside house and temporarily LARP their return to a more "simple" and "trad" cottage core lifestyle. Most of us had to reconsider technology and more specifically the World Wide Web as public space.

While the great blizzard of 1978 is what allowed the invention of the Computerised Bulletin Board System (CBBS), the COVID-19 pandemic accelerated online community formations of a new kind, facilitated by the affordances of a relatively opaque and enclosed ecosystem of group coordination platforms as their users attempt to exit both the financially profitable polarizing nature of mainstream social media, and its censorship.

Sam Hart, Laura Lotti, and Toby Shorin note in their essay "Squad Wealth" that "mass social media are hazardous PvP (Player vs Player) zones no one should traverse without team support." I happened to find such a support within what constitutes Venkatesh Rao's "CozyWeb" or Yancey Strickler's "Dark Forest" ecosystems, depending on who's definition we most align with. Essentially, what they both attempt to describe is a part of the internet that is not indexed by search engines and free from the gravity of our contemporary algorithmic web browsing experience. Think of the apps Discord, Slack, Substack, Urbit, Telegram, and other web 2.5 semi-private message boards and chat-rooms.

Yancey Strickler describes them as spaces where "depressurized conversation is possible because of their non-indexed, non-optimized, and non-gamified environments," to which he adds that "the cultures of those spaces have more in common with the physical world than the internet." Interviews I've conducted through the last months of 2021 with active members of online communities I myself take part in revealed how the changing nature of cities and the progressive erasure of public spaces have too played a role in Dark Forest landscape development.

> "Cities are becoming toxic factories of isolation. We think we live in cities, but they've been mutating into malls. Public spaces, or third places like local cafes in European cities are dead in most of North America. Los Angeles is a perfect example of how the last century of urban planning and zoning committees have created hostile sprawl. Chat communities are just a different type of that good cafe vibe, a hang out space that real cities have lost."

> Redacted, Personal Interview

Now home to your average far right extremist, shitcoiner, gamer, cultural producer, etc, Discord ("Imagine a Place"™ — originally "Your place to talk and hang out"™) was launched in 2015 two years after Slack ("Where work happens™"). The taglines are self-explanatory. The former puts an emphasis on community and leisure and the latter does so on work and productivity, but both platforms essentially exist at the intersection of play and labor and what, in this year working from home, is really the difference anyway?

After nearly a year spent inside both my house and inside these freshly formed communities, I reached out to Caroline Busta — co-founder of New Models (NM), a media platform and community addressing the emergent effects of networked technology on culture — in November 2020 to discuss one of those ideas you get on your way to work and most likely forget as soon as you arrive: since we never really know how long the party will last — remember MySpace? — could there be some way to precipitate the traces of this year spent extremely online? How could we archive, but also distribute (with context) the ideas and experiences shared on the New Models Discord server?

After a quick chat and an announcement posted on the #nm-yearbook break out channel, the CodexCru — a more or less liquid working group composed (mainly) of Attila Haraszti, Jak Ritger, Matïss Groskaufmanis, Orla Tiffney, @phm, Rosie Overell, Sarah Wambold, Will Freudenheim, and myself — got together for the first time on November 25th to share initial thoughts and to discuss what a 2020 NM yearbook, now CODEX Y2K20, could or should be. What followed was a collaboration of roughly seven months of weekly meetings, group calls, and asynchronous chats digging up "old" threads, links, pictures, and memes in an attempt to make sense of it all.

If that meant spending hours navigating spreadsheets and deliberating on X, Y, and Z, it also meant building trust, emotional bonds, and relationships through shared experiences that otherwise have been rather scarce. As I often like to recall with a humorous tone, we literally spent New Year's Eve together online, as doing anything else didn't seem all that safe at that point.

In parallel to this project and a few weeks after CodexCru swapped avatars and handles for real faces and government names, Do Not Research (DNR) — a collaborative publishing platform tracking the development of online

At this point, it feels as though the world

will more likely end with a bid than a bang

subcultures—was seeded by the participants of the reading group organized within the Super Secret Sleeper Cell, a Discord community founded by artist Joshua Citarella. I'm mentioning DNR in part due to my involvement, but also because I believe that both the NM Codex and DNR share a common and particularly contemporary media form: they are both byproducts of "creator-to-fan" networks and other paid communities resulting from the economic model enabled by crowdfunding services such as Patreon.

That said, none of the digital undergrowth would have germinated if we didn't have "the best win conditions," to quote my friend Abbey: that is, a community willing to build and a culture of encouraging dialogue, care, and co-operation for creating some other kind of normal or non-normal. If you had the chance to peek into the late 'Incellectuals' (RIP) server—hell on earth but on Discord— you'd know that much more than people and a "server" is needed to make an inhabitable digital space.

As some of these communities, including NM with its Codex and the SSSC with DNR now reveal themselves to be extremely generative but also collaborative by nature, it's only fair to ask how they should be governed and their resources managed in order not to repeat the extractive and pyramidal labor structure of the cultural field and other Art Worlds people inhabiting these spaces decided to partly retire from to begin with.

In a paper titled "Admin, Mods, and Benevolent dictators for life," writer and researcher Nathan Schneider explores the implicit feudalism of contemporary online platforms and communities as he asks: "When was the last time you participated in an election for a Facebook Group, or sat on a jury for a GitHub project?" He traces back this legacy to the BBS era by quoting interviewees from BBS: The Documentary reminding us that "ultimately the sysop possessed a form of total authority because they lived under the same roof as the host PC. In a moment of frustration, the sysop could always pull the plug and shut down the whole system."

As some pockets of digital culture now gradually explore Web3 (communities and networks built on blockchain-based distributed ledger technologies), we find ourselves caught between two fires: promises of distributed governance and shared ownership, freed from the feudal legacies of Web1 on one end, and the financialization of EVERYTHING on the other. Yet there are still scams at every corner and, at this point, it feels as though the world will more likely end with a bid than a bang.

While the speculative engine attracts both more capital and people, making new (very much needed) experiments possible, projects inscribing themselves within the "decentralized" logic of Web3 often borrow—when they don't co-opt—the language and strategies of solidarity-based economics through the promise of shared and collective ownership. In the context of the publishing platform Mirror, allow me to sincerely ask WTF does: "Joining Mirror does not only make you a community member. It makes you a co-owner of the platform. As a result, our platform is a sum of our contributors" even mean?!?

All jokes aside, Mirror as a platform does develop potentially useful and open source tooling for fundraising, ownership distribution, and resource allocation in the realm of publishing. In the meantime, the promises of many if not most Web3 projects, as in the case of Mirror, often remain vague and hard to visualize through more concrete terms, and could as well hide behind the jargon a future as bleak as the one that the so-called "Sharing Economy" held for us.

In 2014, Vitalik Buterin, co-founder of the Ethereum blockchain, introduced the concept of Decentralized Autonomous Organizations, or DAOs, in an article titled DAOs, DACs, DAs and More: An Incomplete Terminology Guide. He then described them as entities that operate based on coded protocols validated on the blockchain, with a primary focus on automation and a reduced role for human input.

When speaking of democratically governed and collectively owned organizational forms, Decentralized Autonomous Organizations (DAOs) seem to have become the new go-to solution and/or alternative to the traditional cooperative model.

While the latter is bound to geographical constraints and governmental regulations, the former is translocal by nature and operates in a legislative grey area. Moving beyond good and evil, advertising slogans, and blockchain-enabled dystopian fictions, we can hopefully still see value in the potential and affordances of what for now, with no fully automated whatever in sight, is essentially a "group chat with a shared bank account."

While governance mechanisms are discussed at length within communities centered around blockchain based technologies, DAOs as they currently function embody an implicit paradoxical tension leading to frictions between two of its main components or building blocks:

1. Off-chain governance mediated via the informal nature of modes of communication at play within web 2.5 group coordination platforms such as discord or slack—now a foundational layer of what we can call the 'DAO Stack'.

2. A search for radical transparency and other protocol based forms of democratic (on-chain) governance automated through smart contracts.

If on-chain governance often takes the form of proposals open to all and voted on by the members, off-chain governance is much more implicit and goes way beyond the debates and seemingly casual chat taking place on the "public" forum. It moves from the Proof of Work bingo to the Proof of Vibes lingo which in its own way too ensures the security of the network by rendering legible who belongs and who doesn't, insiders and outsiders.

In "Squad Wealth," Other Internet define vibes as "the ineffable energy that the squad values most" and "an unstable substance of high information density." Online communities, very much like their IRL counterpart, do operate on "vibes." Vibes always be shifting, and for those who do not live in the pod and do not eat the bugs, virtual community lore moves much faster than one can keep track of.

> "Lore is history, myth and knowledge on a smaller scale. It permeates laterally through a community, being regulated and disseminated by a centralized body as objective fact. Lore becomes an alternative to mainstream sources of information, be they journalistic, corporate, or governmental. It is in-group knowledge that becomes the backbone of subculture."
>
> Libby Marrs & Tiger Dingsun, The Lore Zone

Wanting to dive deeper into these questions, in November 2021 I invited the researcher Nathan Schneider to discuss the topics addressed in this text.

<u>Leïth Benkhedda (LB):</u> How are you experiencing the current and sudden interest in blockchains and more specifically DAOs?

<u>Nathan Schneider (NS):</u> I was hanging around during the early developments of Ethereum in 2014. It was mostly speculative at that point as in something you could talk about but not necessarily do. Now the question is rather: are we really doing it? Is it enough to have a Discord and a token? Is Discord too centralized? As with most "crypto" stuff my feeling is that it's all really bad, depressing, and uninspiring, but some of the things happening in the middle of it somehow redeems it all.

You have some people who are doing experiments in democracy and self-governance that the world really needs in order to shake the paradigm we've been stuck in in terms of corporate structures, states, and these kinds of entities. A lot of it is obviously filled by money. But if this is what brings people in and allows experimentations to happen I'm glad to see it, though I'll always remain concerned of to whom this is benefiting.

<u>LB:</u>   In your book Everything for Everyone you discuss how the cooperative movement has been erased from history. I've personally become interested in co-ops through a first interest in DAOs. Do you believe that there is a return of the concept of communality?

<u>NS:</u>   There are some really important distinctions to make as this mix at times makes me a little nervous. For example, people have compared Occupy Wall Street, which I wrote a book on and was very involved with, to GameStop.
In my opinion these are complete opposites. Yes, they both have some indignant attitude towards financial firms, but that's where the similarity ends. One is focused on speculation and the useless game of high finance, while another is about feeding people in the streets.
This difference is essential. One has to be careful not to conflate DAOs and co-ops.
The Anglophone Cooperative movement in England came out of a political movement meant to enfranchise working class people. Part of the rationale for building these mini-democracies was to show that working class people could be democratic subjects, and that their project was intertwined with a political vision.
At times what goes by the name of a community is just a bunch of people with a token trying to make the line go up, but there is a way in which economics can have the ability to transcend itself. People enter these spaces and build

culture together, and some of the things I've figured out in parts of my research is that if some people are first coming for the money, they often end up staying for something else. We are starting to see an evolution where people are recognizing the need for reliance on something else. I'm not too hopeful that our problems are going to solve themselves. There is a deep danger of profound and dystopian financialization at work in these tools. But there is also the possibility of something else.

LB: We often speak of "barrier to entry" and the difficulty to onboard people into the blockchain ecosystem. It could be due to the technical vocabulary, jargon, or simply a financial issue. But the bureaucratic processes one needs to engage with for creation and the management of an organization built on cooperative principles can't be seen as really simple either.

NS: On the one hand we are seeing DAOs incorporated as co-ops particularly here in Colorado. It helps solve a problem for DAOs since legal structures are necessary for anything that resembles a business. It's something that I've been exploring for years and it's finally starting to happen. That's one side of it. On the other, co-ops are having the opposite problem of DAOs as in many ways they suffer from capital constraints. Co-ops have been systematically disempowered in many societies. They don't have the access to capital that other kinds of business have.

Community ownership has been treated as this dangerous thing we need to outlaw and constrain in very particular ways, while part of the appeal with DAOs is that there is all this token magic money flowing around. But the more I see and interact with people who are building the plane as they fly it, the more I see them starting to ask questions like what can we learn from co-ops in order to do things right? What can we learn from these legacies? Unfortunately the answers are kind of boring: they usually have a board, an annual meeting, elections. DAOs have the tools to play around with these old conventions. This is something the world of co-ops really needs.

There is a real opportunity for convergence, where both sides meet each other in some respects, and I can imagine a situation where at the end we have a wide range of DAOs: the DAOs which resemble more investor-driven things, all about numbers, and other DAOs which identify with the co-operative principle and see themselves as part of that culture. In so many ways co-ops have completely lost their founding superpower of mutual relationship among members. They've become bureaucratized and slightly less dangerous organizations. Both the culture and tech around DAOs introduces this possibility for the co-op movement to re-discover what made it so powerful to begin with.

LB: Speaking of bureaucracy, there is a tension that I find particularly interesting within tokenized communities: the obsession for transparency and protocol-based forms of governance and the interpersonal dimension of such spaces which often creates more implicit and charisma-oriented forms of leadership echoing the governance structure of some of the '70s communes.

NS: I tend to lean towards Jo Freeman's tyranny of structurlessness, the idea that when you see a group of any significance running on vibes, it's simply an oligarchy. Maybe these communities are based on charisma and people don't care. But if people are expecting accountability and are being told that they are getting it but aren't, it's a problem.

LB: In "Admin, Mods, and Benevolent Dictators for Life," you explored the legacy of BBS systems and how the infrastructure for contemporary online communities set us up for "implicit feudalism." Is Web3 really any different?

<u>NS:</u>　I think DAOs finally break that and I give them a lot of credit for it. Even federated networks still follow a certain feudal logic. Our community is now on a network, and distribution of power is actually what allows us to grow. It's actually the first time technology is finally nudging us outside of that feudalism. It's a very important shift and the gravity of that opportunity is immense.

<u>LB:</u>　During a panel discussion about NFTs, Hito Steyerl asked, "What happens when everything becomes a DAO, where are the hospitals?" Blockchains allow for third party free translocal distribution of resources which can be incredibly powerful but only because they are built on what I see as a Libertarian Paradise or Hellscape. Do you see such benefit as worth the losses they might engender?

<u>NS:</u>　During the Bitcoin era, I used to ask people are you sure you want to get rid of the Federal Reserve for this thing that constantly fluctuates? These technologies, as with the web, were distributed technologies that produced the most centralized companies the world has ever seen. Blockchains can do those things even more, and we need to recognize the dangers we are walking into as well as the possibilities. We should always ask what can we learn from the past and honor things like a national health system. Those are great gifts. Let's build on these legacies and deep histories to ground us in this crazy speculative moment.

02.08.2021

Moving Castles:
Modular and Portable Multiplayer Miniverses
by Arthur Röing Baer and GVN908

A Moving Castle — as popularized by Studio Ghibli's cult movie *Howl's Moving Castle*, based on Diana Wynne Jones' 1986 book of the same title — is a nomadic patchwork of different spaces of mutating and incoherent scale. Such spaces are "bespelled to hold together" by the will of their inhabitants, which the Moving Castle can transport to different worlds in times of needs or wish.

> "With a last squeak the castle lifted, the crew cheered as we could see across the dark forest for the first time, our eyes locked on the arid wastelands on the horizon. Now back to chat, this machine won't move itself"

In our vision of this new media format, Moving Castles are modular and portable multiplayer miniverses inhabited by communities that use them to manage their lore, ecosystems, and economies. With this first post, we sketch their blueprints and collage the new collectively produced media-format that can emerge from within Moving Castles. After collecting the seeds from which these communities could grow and sustain themselves, we'll finally take a look at how they can be built and how to facilitate an exchange with a public outside their familiar territories.

1/5 Not islands or dark forests, but vehicles

We are part of Trust, a knowledge-community that lives on a member-restricted Discord. The focus over the last year has been on producing online events which take shape as Collective Reading Groups, Sandbox (a combined voice and chat presentation format), and publicly available streams and talks on Twitch.

Trust and a large variety of other semi-private communities — from pay-to-enter-Discords, game guilds, blockchain communities, subscription-mediated newsletters, and group chats — are what Yancey Strickler calls Dark Forests. According to him these are "spaces where depressurized conversation is possible because of their non-indexed, non-optimized, and non-gamified environments." Ribbonfarm's Venkatesh Rao has another term for it: "the Cozyweb works on the (human) protocol of everybody cutting-and-pasting bits of text, images, URLs, and screenshots across live streams." Where Dark Forests are characterized by their intentional withdrawal from social media, the Cozyweb is non-indexable because of a lacking interconnection between material, creating unintentionally disconnected islands populated by isolated communities.

In spite of their differences in intentionality, both terms describe communities that withdraw themselves from participation in the power laws of social platforms. According to New Models' Carly Busta, and Do Not Research's Joshua Citarella, it is through this withdrawal that these new subcultures find the space to develop shared interests and build their collective lore.

What we believe to be most promising about emerging spaces like Trust is their potential to grow into collectively owned social and cultural institutions built on decentralized infrastructure: democratically governed manifestations of collective interest ranging from political aims to fandoms,

contributed to and run by their members.

The characterization of these communities as isolated islands or dark forests, while useful in describing our current media landscape, sits uneasily with both our experience of participating in Trust, and our hopes for these spaces developing into democratic social institutions which have a relationship and responsibility to the public. As a recent post by Laura Lotti, Sam Hart, and Toby Shorin points out, we need new articulations of how decentralized online communities interact with the public, and attached conceptions of the public good, one that as they put forward, should be framed around positive externalities rather than internal interests. Therefore we believe there is a risk for communities embracing isolating metaphors such as the Dark Forest. Such an embrace could lead to these communities developing similarly to the historical precedent of merchant guilds: rent-seeking online tribes that optimize for internal value creation but with little to no concept of responsibility to the outside or a similar notion of other publics.

As we collectively figure out how to facilitate and evaluate positive externalities, there needs to be possibility for involvement, participation, and exchange with other groups and potential future stakeholders; a public outside the dark forest.

2/5 A New Route to the Outside

If we do not involve a public, we risk institutionalizing an understanding of collectivity that only includes and reinforces one's own tribe while furthering collective (often financial) interests — all happening under the false belief that echo chambers are somehow a valid form of political or social engagement.

We will now look at the media currently used to facilitate exchange between these private communities and external publics. To what extent are these dominant media models capable of producing positive externalities? And to what extent might their current affordances be counter-productive to long-term visions of collective agency and public participation expressed in the desire for decentralized and democratic institutions?

Currently, many semi-private communities that rely on crowdfunding to finance their activities also use the public media formats of the creator economy, or Clearnet Stadiums; a vast array of podcasts, private newsletters, and video-essays built to highlight individual sensibilities and passions. Creator Stadiums give expression to the thoughts and knowledge of the content-creators that use them to communicate with potential and already existing audiences. This sharing of media formats between dark forest communities and Clearnet Stadiums can be traced to their shared emergence on a certain generation of mid-2010s tech platforms such as Patreon, Discord, Substack, and their reliance on the crowdfunding mechanisms that lie at the core of these platforms.

Carly Busta and Lil Internet refer to the relationship between these communities and the tech platforms used for public visibility as the interplay between Dark Forests and Clearnet. It is the moving between Dark Forests and Clearnet which makes sheltered conversation and fermentation possible, whilst making the emergent ideas part of a larger discourse that allows new people to discover, critique, or join the project to contribute and decide on internal and public activities.

As New Models point out, clearnet platforms are the next-best thing dark forest communities currently have to facilitate interactions with a public, due to their discoverability and low-barrier participation. That private platforms such as Amazon's Twitch, Twitter, and Facebook now constitute the digital equivalents to public spheres is as much a political failure as one of our collective imagination.

As the two trajectories of stadiums and their potentially decentralized counterparts progress, we predict that the media and tooling built for the first will be more evidently incompatible with the goals of the second. Certain types of media are ideal for stadiums that have influencers at the heart of their activity, and some media forms are better suited to decentralized institutions with many contributors: a megaphone is not a great tool for having everyone's voice heard, podcasts are not interactive formats, and video-essays are (currently) not produced together with the audience.

In result, there is an emerging need to supplement new distributed funding and decentralized governance mechanisms with new routes between private communities and public participation. We need new participatory media formats, as well as changes to existing formats, to better represent and facilitate collective agency and value distribution so that communities can avoid exactly the effects they are trying to escape from — Web 2.0 influencer dynamics and their power laws where all the value and control flows to a few central nodes. We think of these private platforms as arid wastelands that still need to be ventured into for loot, the rescue of new members, and the building of our new vehicles, until we can replace them with decentralized alternatives.

3/5 Moving Castles

In order to be a viable alternative to clearnet stadiums, Moving Castles must reflect the following principles. The principles are adapted from the design goals described in Modular Politics:

1. Collective: Many contributors share control through transparent and real-time governance mechanisms.

Map inspired by the Eghbal model of open-source communities,
"Working in Public: The Making and Maintenance of Open Source Software"
Nadia Eghbal (2020).
↓

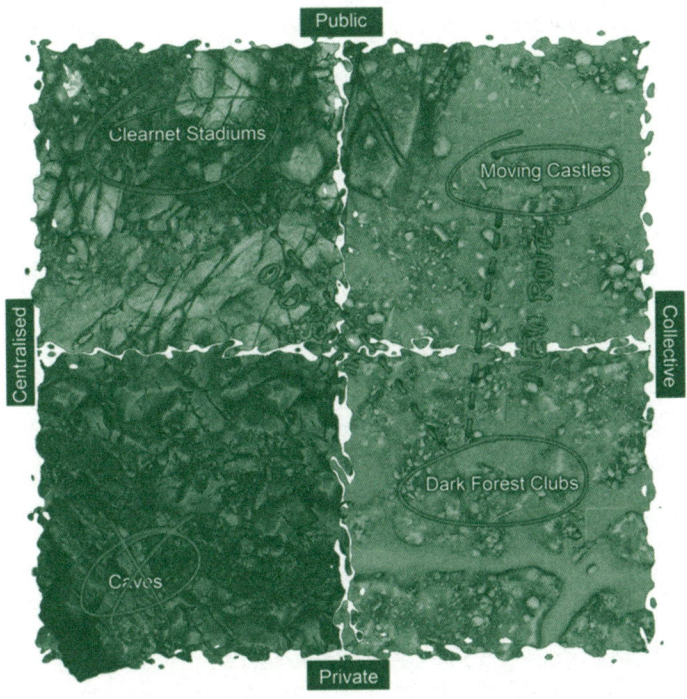

Arthur Röing Baer & GVN908   CH.2 Moving Castles

2. Portable: To avoid lock-in mechanisms, Moving Castles have the ability to move freely between platforms, standards, and protocols, from private to public, without losing any value, knowledge, or lore in the process.

3. Modular: Communities should have the ability to construct Moving Castles by creating, importing, and arranging composable parts (such as avatars, props, and environments) together as a coherent whole while making these parts available for others to reuse and adapt.

4. Interoperable: They have the ability to interact with other communities; communicating, playing games, and sharing knowledge and skills in order to help these communities become Moving Castles themselves.

Each moving castle can be thought of as a miniverse inhabited and controlled by a community through a number of inputs. Compared to the generalized idea of the metaverse in which one persistent and shared virtual reality allows for much less customization on a community level, a miniverse is flexible, adaptable, and agile. In this way, a Moving Castle's structure can be thought of as a mix of a Discord server and a Massive Multiplayer Online game (MMO). And, similarly to a Discord server, a Moving Castle has a main space subdivided into rooms or channels, each composed of a theme, lores, rules, and potential mechanisms.

> "Through magic the door is connected to doorways in other locations, effectively making a door with one interior and several possible exteriors, allowing the wizard(s) to travel anywhere they establish a connection and to easily return home while traveling."

In Wynne-Jones' book (and in Miyazaki's movie) the doors of the Moving Castle are portals that lead to a variety of

Sketch of a Moving Castle made up of modules, with additional character design by Parr Geng.
↓

changing worlds and contexts. In our miniverse, the doors enable a variety of changing inputs and outputs, from APIs to communication with other Moving Castles. For example, doors that enable web3 integration would allow Moving Castles to become a representative media of DAOs and Multisigs, controlled by members with the inclusion and visualization of financial mechanisms and the ability to read and write directly from and to permissionless ledgers. By integrating subscriptions or token access for roles, it becomes possible to circumvent services like Patreon and Twitch subscriptions to source funds, while also allowing far greater portability to future decentralized alternatives (that are already emerging). Other doors could lead to friendly communities, allowing free movement of users, items, and lore between the castles.

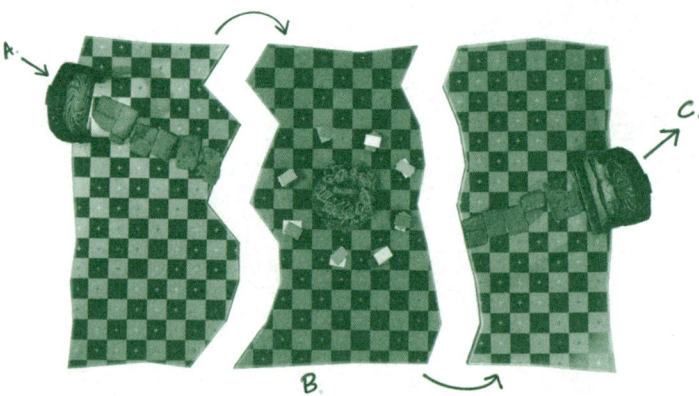

Moving Castles allow the interchangeable combination of parts in a modular fashion, such as, for example: A) raw API inputs B) collective governance such as voting C) resulting web3 outputs.

Full customizability is achieved by using real-time rendering softwares, such as Unreal Engine. These allow the community to commission, create, or reshape the components of their Moving Castle themselves. As a result, Moving Castles are not hermetically sealed, self-ossifying spaces, but instead can be swapped, combined, and merged in a modular fashion. This scrappy, constantly re-assembling amalgamation of rooms, mechanisms, community members, and portal doors is what we define as a Moving Castle.

As Moving Castles progress in development, a fifth principle might be added to our list of defining criteria: persistence. Persistent miniverses would allow Moving castles to become alive through continuous gameplay, evolving world-states, unstructured social interactions, lore libraries, and idle-games for community members at any time.

Moving Castles float in the intertidal zone between public and private waters while providing tools for portable self-organization. By adding more functionalities to Moving Castles and combining them using our modular structures, we hope to see a Cambrian explosion of new egregores — monsters, biospheres, mega-cities, flying machines, and vehicles — all built for specific goals and governed by their respective communities and stakeholders. This in turn could lay the foundation for a network of interoperable Moving Castles, all communicating, playing games, and bumping into each other — steered by the shouts of their respective communities.

> "We are moving from an era of centralized, bureaucratic value creation firms to an era of decentralized, permissionless value creation networks. As organizational models change, so too will the intangible cultural artifacts created by these new institutional forms. Brands, narratives, memes— we now choose our own headless gods."

There needs to be possibility for involvement, participation and exchange

with other groups and potential future stakeholders, a public outside the dark forest

Arthur Röing Baer & GVN908

CH.2 Moving Castles

Having now sketched out our vision for what Moving Castles could be, we now turn to the question of how to bring them into existence.

4/5 Kitbashed Castles in the Sky

Over the past year, we produced a series of livestreamed media experiments to test the framework of Moving Castles and develop foundational layers of their infrastructure. Developed using Unreal Engine and hosted on Twitch, our Mascot Streams explored new types of collective agency and encouraged community participation using game design and interactive mechanics.

Our Mascot Streams mixed elements of game shows,

reading groups, and networked knowledge production, all facilitated in a 3D game world by a motion-captured mascot. The audience could interact with and control objects, avatars, and environments through chat-inputs in real-time. Each stream explored parallels between economic and game mechanisms, using those same game mechanics to trigger the reading and discussion of research and writing on new and strange economic forms and phenomena. Each stream additionally tackled a different experiment in interaction design, aimed at allowing for collective involvement in play and worldbuilding through Twitch, from live gambling via chat to in-stream viewer representation.

In our streams we tested a series of experimental functions relating to the underlying infrastructure of our prototypical Moving Castle:

1. Real-time motion capture of Mascot(s), directly controlled by streamer/author (face and body movements, content of event) and indirectly by audience (appearance)

2. Remote control of UE4 world (mascot, props and environment with imbued mechanisms) by audience via Twitch chat (governance)

3. Audience embodied presence in world through 3D avatars controlled by chat-inputs

4. Persistent tokens used to unlock characters, interactions, and alternative storylines

In all of these experiments, it was necessary to embrace a strategy of kitbashing, a practice in model building and 3D graphics whereby a new model is created by taking pieces out of commercial kits. In lieu of a fully customizable metaverse; a collective virtual shared space where communities can interact virtually while controlling the economic and programmatic logics at the core of their interactions, we have bootstrapped our Moving Castles by combining existing participatory elements and reach from Twitch live-streaming with the modular customizability of game engines.

In doing so, our streams drew inspiration from a broader current of social experiments such as Twitch Plays Pokémon, created by an anonymous Australian programmer in 2014, in which Twitch users control a character writing game-inputs directly into the chat collectively puppeteering the gameplay through a very crude form of direct democracy known as anarchy mode.

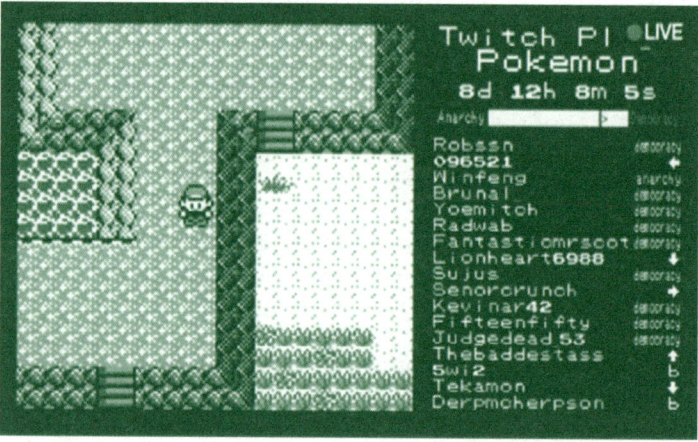

Twitch Plays Pokémon demonstrates how game design that facilitates collective coordination can create alternatives to centralized and authored narratives. We took this as a starting point to think about more complex forms of control, input, and output to lay the foundation for a media type that can combine collective agency with public participation, all while using (and subverting) the tools offered by an existing platform.

Looking a little further back in media history, formats such as the Danish "live one-player multi-platform interactive game show" HUGO, first broadcast in 1990, managed to successfully exploit a series of existing infrastructures. Using video game consoles, national TV, and landline phones to create a new hybrid format, an audience of young gamers could call in via land-line and control a live-streamed game on their TV using their phones as remote gamepads enabling the interaction with the not-yet manifested future of online games.

In the absence of an infrastructure that can function as the foundation for the construction of Moving Castles, and taking inspiration from Twitch Plays Pokémon and HUGO, we propose to kitbash new miniverses using a similar form of hybrid media that combines the participation of Twitch live-streaming with game engines. The resulting miniverses are small and independent worlds inhabited and used by communities which already today accept the tradeoffs of simple- and high-latency inputs in favor of customizable, fun, and participatory media.

We believe these streams can point at how decentralized narrative production can bridge false divisions between content-consumers and creators by rethinking how media can be produced collectively. Although authored content still plays an important role in these formats, it functions more like raw material for the audience to manipulate. We found that by giving agency to the audience we made it possible for them to take the event into uncharted territories. This brings forward interesting questions of how to balance authorship and community interest, a question we want to explore further in future streams by building more complex mechanics to test different types of collective agency.

5/5 Who is Steering?

"Heroes are powerful. Before you know it, the men and women in the wild-oat patch and their kids and the skills of the makers and the thoughts of the thoughtful and the songs of the singers are all part of it, have all been pressed into service in the tale of the Hero. But it isn't their story. It's his"

The Carrier Bag Theory of Fiction, URSULA K. LE GUIN

Whereas Joseph Campbell's mythological concept of the Hero's Journey was the trademark of an era of authored and linear media production, Moving Castles and similar participatory stream formats that are governed and built by thousands of players/agents could become emblematic of a rhizomatic and decentralized approach to narrative production native to real-time rendered media, that is, (paraphrasing Umberto Eco's words on the Opera Aperta) a type of media that rather than presenting itself in a well-defined and closed manner to its audience, pre-scripted by its composer: "reject the definitive, concluded message and multiply the formal possibilities of the distribution of their elements." They offer themselves not as finite works which prescribe specific repetition along given structural coordinates but as "open" works, which are brought to their conclusion by the audience at the same time as she experiences them on an aesthetic plane.

As Twitch Plays Pokémon grew, the need for more complex governance mechanisms to facilitate collective coordination were implemented and anarchy mode was supplemented with democracy mode. Democracy mode, as the name suggests, averaged inputs rather than following them directly, creating a more coordinated (and some suggest, boring) end result. These learnings, together with other streams such as Built a Trading Bot to let Subscribers Trade $25,000 on Twitch which expand collective agency to also affect external processes, further point towards how an extension of these narrative formats through more complex governance mechanisms — such as those developed by Trust's own Black Swan and described in Modular Politics — can turn simple user inputs into sophisticated outputs that interact with a number of external APIs and web3 protocols.

This combination of decentralized and real time authorship that can influence external processes enables Moving Castles' collectively authored narratives to also function as community dashboards for collective governance and stakeholder events. Time-specific formats for engaging low-barrier governance over digital commons and decentralized communities.

Moving Castles are collective machines controlled by governance mechanisms and allow low-barrier participation. They are modular so that they can be customized by communities and parts can be shared between them. By kitbashing Moving Castles from already existing game engines and live-streaming platforms we can build them now while ensuring portability, and through pursuing interoperability point towards a federation of Moving Castles linked together.

A network of Moving Castles allows us to escape binary thinking of dark forests and clearnets to instead think about many publics as one network. Many organizational miniverses coming together inside one or many interoperable multiverse(s); larger constellations of Moving Castles. Here, communities themselves define the social and technical rules at the core of their institutions while coming together through a federated model to exchange, trade, disagree, and collaborate.

Our experiments thus far have barely scratched the surface of the new types of narrative works that combine low-barrier public participation with collective agency. We hope to see similar experiments by other communities moving towards decentralized institutions that are financed, owned, and governed by their own members. With Moving Castles we aim to have presented both an organizational metaphor and one of several very needed media-formats to support this development.

Thank you to the participants of the collective reading group who through their input and ideas vastly improved this piece.

A special thanks to @thejaymo @duster @Son La @bunkerheadz1998 @muein @calsbot @haywirez @arp d @Joanna @ráchel @parrr @nickh @wassim.

We also want to thank Other Internet Peer Review for their important insights and feedback which helped shape the piece to what it is today. A special thanks to Jay Springett, Kara Kittel, Toby Shorin, Laura Lotti, Sam Hart, Bryan Lehrer, John Palmer, Callil Capuozzo & Kei Kreutler.

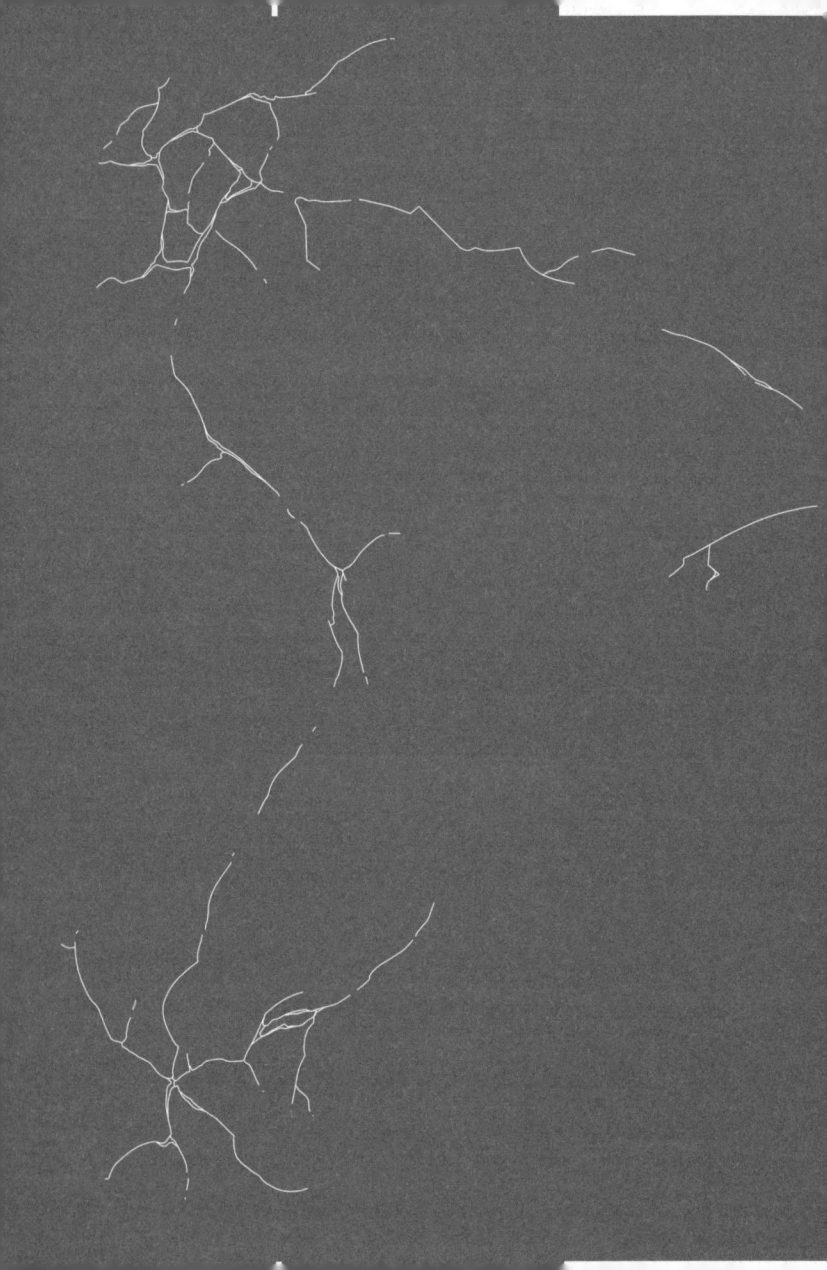

THE DARK FOREST ERA

III

14.01.2021

The internet didn't kill counterculture
You just won't find it on Instagram
by Caroline Busta

Search Google Images for "counterculture" and it overwhelmingly returns black-and-white photos of young people all now over 60. In the pictures, it is so clear what they were countering: The Man, of course, who, with his white collar, white skin, and short hair, singlehandedly symbolized dominant cultural norms. In the age of social media, personal expression has become the most valuable form of currency, yet we still use the term "counterculture" to describe alternatives to the hegemonic forces of yesteryear, as if dressing middle-class, white, and preppy still aligned with the rules of power today.

In an era more profoundly organized by Big Tech than our own elected governments, the new culture to be countered isn't singular or top-down. It's rhizomatic, nonbinary, and includes all who live within the Google/Apple/Facebook/Amazon digital ecosystem (aka GAFA stack). With digital platforms transforming legacy countercultural activity into profitable, high-engagement content, being countercultural no longer means being counter-hegemonic. What logic could possibly be upended by punks, goths, gabbers, or neo-pagans when the internet, a massively lucrative space of capitalization, profits off the personal expression and political conflict of its users?

As recently as the early '90s, abjection and extreme

profanity still worked pretty well to repel the big social threats of the time: pearl-clutching conservatives with their anti-progressive ideology and market recuperation. Take, for instance, musician GG Allin in an American-flag loincloth, fighting with his audience and shitting on stage before launching into a performance of "I'm Gonna Rape You," or artist and noise musician Boyd Rice, in what he reports was a prank, joining the founder of the white supremacist group American Front in a 1989 Sassy photo shoot for an article the teen magazine was running on neo-Nazis. In context, these artists (like the psychedelic hippies of yore) were being literally countercultural—using culture against itself to violate the hegemonic push toward, in Allin's and Rice's case, neoliberal "responsibilization."

In today's online space, however, this strategy breaks down. Brought back into the spotlight in 2018 via a NYC gallery exhibition of visually innocuous abstract paintings, Rice quickly found himself at the center of controversy as his decades-old Sassy appearance (among other such stunts) tripped present-day censors. An old punk, he smirked at the outrage. "I'm too dangerous for New York City," he told Artnet. Yet he wasn't too dangerous for the internet. High-tension discussion of his work and life and the gallerist's moral compass raged online, which is to say Rice was attentionally successful online. Despite being informed by billions, this new technological hegemony isn't democratic; it's a swarm-led form of para-governance programmed to maximize engagement while obfuscating responsibility for the social and environmental damage it wreaks. Zuckerberg, Bezos, Thiel, and other tech behemoths are quick to remind us that they're not in charge of public laws or policy — their empires were built according to the "peaceful mechanisms" of free-market capitalism — and that society has adopted their tools and spaces through its own free will. If pressed, they'll point out how their platforms reflect the countercultural demands of earlier

Caroline BustaCH.3 The Internet Didn't Kill Counterculture

generations: eschewing big government and vertical corporate culture while encouraging personal fulfillment and flat organizational structures. Today you can be a coder and a DJ, an Uber driver and a travel blogger, a Sand Hill Road suit and a Robot Heart Burner.

Similarly slippery is the new look of power. Far from the parades, palaces, and outsize girths of present-day strongmen like Viktor Orbán, Kim Jong-un, and Donald Trump, the most iconic tells you'll find among the big tech set are more likely to be a black turtleneck, a Patagonia fleece, and the absence of carrying bags. It's a flex to be visually indistinguishable from the crowd. The power of today is firmly situated in minimalism, restraint, and ease — it's only power under threat that turns to physical displays of strength. Actual power is controlling the means by which lesser power can be displayed — i.e., congrats on the 500K likes on your polling numbers, @jack* (now @elon) still owns all your tweets. Actual power keeps a low profile. Actual power doesn't need a social media presence, it owns social media.

In recent years, users have started to register this shift. Yet the term counterculture still gets used to describe someone like rapper Tekashi 6ix9ine, whose notoriety — first breaking society's code (sexual abuse and murder conspiracy, among other offenses) and then the omertà code of the streets (snitching on fellow gang members to lessen his own sentence) — propelled him to superstardom. "Gooba," a track he surprise-dropped upon being surprise-released from prison, made YouTube history by becoming the most-watched rap video in a 24-hour span, frying the platform's view counter. That same day, 2 million simultaneous users tuned in to his Instagram Live as he confessed into his phone camera: "I snitched, I ratted. But who was I supposed to be loyal to?" And then with a sparkle of VVS diamonds, "I broke the YouTube. I'm at 5 million views in one hour. [...] A rat is doin' more numbers than you. Numbers don't lie." But behind 6ix9ine's self-loyalty is an unwitting loyalty to the platform and, by extension, to the shareholders of Alphabet and Facebook, Inc. And this is where it gets tricky. To be truly countercultural today, in a time of tech hegemony, one has to, above all, betray the platform, which may come in the form of betraying or divesting from your public online self.

6ix9ine is subcultural, but he isn't countercultural. Someone like Edward Snowden, by comparison, isn't subcultural but may be the closest we get to a countercultural figure in the postdigital age. A US government subcontractor with access to classified intelligence, Snowden saw Big Tech's radically scaling power and, in 2013, exposed the NSA's illegal agreements with major tech platforms to intercept the private e-mail, call records, and cache of "almost anything done on the internet" by users worldwide. Snowden's whistleblowing targeted a major chakra of the new hegemony, resulting in great personal compromise. But a single individual isn't an entire counterculture.

Counterculture requires a group. Us against the world. And the internet is excellent at bringing groups together around collective dissent. But just like the internet, there is nothing inherently socially progressive about these tools. Extinction Rebellion is countercultural in spirit but so too are QAnon, the armed right-wing libertarian Boogaloo Boys, and Europe's Reichsbürger, who deny the existence of present-day Germany, claiming to be citizens of the Third Reich (which, they argue, technically never ended).

A truth specific to our time is that dissent against one level of authority is now very often driven by a deeper hegemonic force. Perhaps this is why, among many younger people (Greta Thunberg notwithstanding), there is less focus on battling current leaders and more interest in divining counter-futures. Instead of attempting to dismantle the master's house using the master's tools, it's more something like: Let's pool crypto to book the master's Airbnb and use the tools we find there to forge a forest utopia that the master could never survive. Central to this counter-future crafting is a strong belief in impending ecological collapse, rendering all the existing systems of control obsolete — which is a logical work-around for thinking about dissent in a time when the socially and ecologically corrosive systems are deemed too sprawling to effectively counter or boycott. Another key factor is Gen Z's rediscovery of PoliticalCompass.org, a Web 1.0 site that, via six sets of prompts with which a user is asked to dis-/identify, generates an approximate position on the Political Compass's X/Y axis of Left to Right, Authoritarian to Libertarian.

Having spent the past several years intensively studying the development of Gen Z's online political expression, artist Joshua Citarella points to the emergence of "e-deologies, radical politics as a form of niche personal branding." In his 2019 report "20 Interviews," Citarella underscores the influence of Political Compass and gaming more generally on ideations of countercultural participation — or what he refers to as a "choose your character / choose your future" mode of "identity play that gained heightened relevance as American politics subsumed all of pop culture" during the mid-2010s.

Among the political identities one finds in this space is, for example: "Ted was right" anarcho-primitivism (anprim), which, following Ted Kaczynski's Industrial Society and Its Future manifesto, promotes a reactionary return to pre-agrarian times where people, reskilled as hunters and gatherers, are no longer alienated from their labor and seek fulfillment through daily survival. If you think this sounds fringe, consider the 10.3 million users currently subscribed to the Primitive Technology channel on YouTube, which has tutorialized building things "in the wild completely from scratch using no modern tools or materials, [...] seeing how far you can go without utilizing modern technology" — except, of course, the device you use to stream the video showing you how.

The names of these e-deologies tend to be both fantastical and literal. A "post-civilizationist" might focus on what optimal human survival would look like were civilization no longer possible. A "voluntarist post-agrarianist," meanwhile, might value anarcho-primitivism skills but see them as integral to realizing a civilization sustained through opt-in agrarian communes. Elsewhere on the compass, one finds the likes of "Fully Automated Luxury Gay Space Communism" (where a total embrace of technology delivers humanity from scarcity, ecological volatility, and the reactionary social ills of resource competition) and the defiantly neo-traditionalist "technocratic theocracy," which puts its faith in a machine-governed future that upholds Christian virtues. E-deologies are further explored on message boards and social media via memes, TikTok posts, and livestreamed Twitch and YouTube debates, all of which can get pretty gnarly (calls for "eco-fash global genocide" and "secession of white ethnostates," etc.) And maybe here, we do have an aesthetic counter to the wallflower non-style of Big Tech: a raging messy semiotic meltdown of radicalizing (if absurdist) meme culture where the only ideological no-go zone is the liberal center. Key here is that most of this activity is happening under the guise of avatars, pseudonyms, and collectively run social media accounts where direct lines between IRL subjects and online personas are rarely clear. The "niche personal branding" is gamified — push an account to the extreme, see what happens. If the platform shuts you down, start over.

While climate change is a shared concern for many younger people, their responses might be more accurately understood as competitive-futurist than countercultural. As the greatly imaginative range of Political Compass positions illustrates, there is little consensus over who or what they are specifically opposing. This is wise in an era when the complexity of global crises makes it exceedingly difficult

To be truly countercultural today, one has to betray the platform which may

come in the form of betraying or divesting from your public online self

Caroline Busta   CH.3 The Internet Didn't Kill Counterculture to effectively isolate responsible parties. How would one even begin to hold, say, Apple accountable for all of the externalities within the life of an iPhone? Who among us could easily give up our connectivity and still be economically and socially okay? It's as if, having grown up on a fully networked Earth, Gen Z has bypassed counterculture, finding it futile in the face of a hegemonic system that more clearly resembles a Hydra than the monolithic forces that legacy counterculture was rebelling against. Intuiting that any activity directly opposing the system will only make the system stronger, the next generation is instead opting for radical hyperstition: constructing alternative futures that abandon our current infrastructure entirely (the emergence of blockchain-based currencies, for instance, or calls to not merely reform but fully abolish the police).

While Citarella's research focuses on teenagers who began posting online around 2016 (and in 2020 are roughly 18 years old), it nevertheless distills the changing nature of contemporary countercultural activity more broadly. For one, anonymity, or at least pseudonymity, is increasingly important if not fundamental to being active online in counter-hegemonic ways. This is very different from, say, 1990s ideations of IRL counterculture, where there was a premium on unmediated authenticity and "being real" (think MTV Unplugged). Now "selling out" is tying your online identity to your IRL life and real name. In part, this is because one of the biggest impediments to countercultural activity is the fact that the internet doesn't suppress expression—it forces you to express and then holds you accountable for whatever you say for years. On the platform, silence isn't an option, at least not if you want the network to remember you exist. This is especially true in the culture sector, where being visible means being kept in mind for gigs and collaborations. There is a reason why 6ix9ine is obsessed with breaking YouTube and why talented young rappers must be equally talented at social media marketing if they ever hope to build a career.

We saw this dynamic metastasize in the wake of George Floyd's murder, when well-intentioned claims of "silence is violence" (recalling the powerful 1987 ACT-UP "Silence = Death" campaign) spiraled into calling out individuals with even a small following who hadn't come forward with a timely public statement of solidarity or remorse. Yet public posts were subject to popular scrutiny and judged based on sincerity, originality, and tone. Not surprisingly, many people defaulted to posting a somber plain black square. But this generated criticism of its own by clogging the feed with an informational blackout during a moment when community resource sharing was critically important. Amid a chaotic time, the platform functioned exactly as designed: amplification of emotions, uptick in user interaction, growth in platform engagement, and data cultivation. Cha-ching, the platform cashes in. What's really messed up about this is that users, despite understanding that the platform's mechanics are net-bad, still feel a moral responsibility to obey the platform-enabled-hive-mind's rules.

On the dark edges of the early internet, hackers foresaw the enclosure of the public commons long before the likes of 6ix9ine, Snowden, and teenage Gen Z. These users developed an ethos that valued the radical freedom of a fully anonymous, hyperconnected zone where people could communicate unburdened by their physical bodies and government names. As online activity began to centralize around search engines, such as Netscape, Explorer, and Google, in the late-'90s and early-'00s, the internet bifurcated into what became known as the "clearnet," which includes all publicly indexed sites (i.e., big social media, commercial platforms, and anything crawled by major search engines) and the "darknet" or "deep web," which is not publicly indexed (due to being built on anonymized, encrypted networks such as Tor). There were also a number of sites that though officially clearnet, laid the groundwork for a sub-clearnet space that we might think of as a "dark forest" zone—particularly message board forums like Reddit and 4chan, where users can interact without revealing their IRL identity or have this activity impact their real-name SEO.

Taken from the title of Chinese sci-fi writer Liu Cixin's 2008 book, "the dark forest" region of the web is becoming increasingly important as a space of online communication for users of all ages and political persuasions. In part, this is because it is less sociologically stressful than the clearnet zone, where one is subject to peer, employer, and state exposure. It also now includes Discord servers, paid newsletters (e.g., Substack), encrypted group messaging (via Telegram, etc.), gaming communities, podcasts, and other off-clearnet message board forums and social media. One forages for content or shares in what others in the community have retrieved rather than accepting whatever the platform algorithms happen to match to your data profile. Additionally, dark forest spaces are both minimally and straightforwardly commercial. There is typically a small charge for entry, but once you are in, you are free to act and speak without the platform nudging your behavior or extracting further value. It is also interesting to keep in mind that the dark forest shares the same cables and satellite arrays as clearnet channels, is accessed via the same devices, and essentially all of its denizens continue to simultaneously participate in clearnet spaces (as contemporary professional protocol demands). It is therefore not analogous to legacy countercultural notions of going off-grid or "dropping out."

To be sure, none of these spaces are pure, and users are just as vulnerable to echo chambers and radicalization in the dark forest as on pop-stack social media. But in terms of engendering more or less counter-hegemonic potential, the dark forest is more promising because of its relative autonomy from clearnet physics (the gravity,

velocity, and traction of content when subject to x algorithm). Unlike influencers and "blue checks," who rely on clearnet recognition for income, status, and even self-worth, dark forest dwellers build their primary communities out of clearnet range — or offline in actual forests, parks, and gardens (e.g., cottagecore and related eco-social trends) — and then only very selectively or even absurdly/incoherently show themselves under clearnet light. The crux of Liu Cixin's book is the creed, when called by the clearnet: "Do not answer! Do not answer!! Do not answer!!! But if you do answer, the source will be located right away. Your planet will be invaded. Your world will be conquered."

So what does today's counter-hegemonic culture look like? It's not particularly interested in being seen — at least not in person. It gets no thrill out of wearing leather and a mohawk and walking past main-street shops, which are empty now anyway. But it does demonstrate a hunger for freedom — freedom from the attention economy, from atomization, and the extractive logic of mainstream communication. We can imagine collectively held physical spaces reclaimed from empty retail or abandoned venues hosting esoteric local scenes, a proliferation of digital gangs in dark forests who hold secrets dear, and a new desire for scarcity in cultural objects — deeper and closer connections made between people even while rejecting the platform's compulsion to "like and share." In the internet era, true counterculture is difficult to see, and even harder to find — but that doesn't mean it's not there.

-

First published in Document Journal, F/W 2020, #17

04.01.2023

The Expanding Dark Forest and Generative AI
by Maggie Appleton

The dark forest theory of the web points to the increasingly life-like but life-less state of being online. Most open and publicly available spaces on the web are overrun with bots, advertisers, trolls, data scrapers, clickbait, keyword-stuffing "content creators," and algorithmically manipulated junk.

It's like a dark forest that seems eerily devoid of human life – all the living creatures are hidden beneath the ground or up in trees. If they reveal themselves, they risk being attacked by automated predators.

Humans who want to engage in informal, unoptimised, personal interactions have to hide in closed spaces like invite-only Slack channels, Discord groups, email newsletters, small-scale blogs, and digital gardens. Or make themselves illegible and algorithmically incoherent in public venues.

That dark forest is about to expand. Large Language Models (LLMs) that can instantly generate coherent swaths of human-like text have just joined the party.

Over the last six months, we've seen a flood of LLM copywriting and content-generation products come out: Jasper, Moonbeam, Copy.ai, and Anyword are just a few. They're designed to pump out advertising copy, blog posts, emails, social media updates, and marketing pages. And they're *really* good at it.

These models became competent copywriters much faster than people expected – too fast for us to fully process the implications. Many people had their come-to-Jesus moment a few weeks ago when OpenAI released ChatGPT, a slightly more capable version of GPT-3 with an accessible chat-bot style interface. The collective shock and awe reaction made clear how few people had been tracking the progress of these models.

To complicate matters, language models are not the only mimicry machines gathering speed right now. Image generators like Midjourney, DALL-E, and Stable Diffusion have been on a year-long sprint. In January they could barely render a low-resolution, disfigured human face. By the autumn they reliably produced images indistinguishable from the work of human photographers and illustrators.

½ A Generated Web

There's a swirl of optimism around how these models will save us from a suite of boring busywork: writing formal emails, internal memos, technical documentation, marketing copy, product announcement, advertisements, cover letters, and even negotiating with medical insurance companies.

But we'll also need to reckon with the trade-offs of making insta-paragraphs and 1-click cover images. These new models are poised to flood the web with generic, generated content.

You thought the first page of Google was bunk before? You haven't seen Google where SEO optimizer bros pump out billions of perfectly coherent but predictably dull informational articles for every longtail keyword combination under the sun.

Marketers, influencers, and growth hackers will set up OpenAI → Zapier pipelines that auto-publish a relentless and impossibly banal stream of LinkedIn #MotivationMonday posts, "engaging" tweet threads, Facebook outrage monologues, and corporate blog posts.

It goes beyond text too: video essays on YouTube, TikTok

clips, podcasts, slide decks, and Instagram stories can all be generated by patchworking together ML systems. And then regurgitated for each medium.

We're about to drown in a sea of pedestrian takes. An explosion of noise that will drown out any signal. Goodbye to finding original human insights or authentic connections under that pile of cruft.

Many people will say we already live in this reality. We've already become skilled at sifting through unhelpful piles of "optimised content" designed to gather clicks and advertising impressions.

4chan proposed dead internet theory years ago: that most of the internet is "empty and devoid of people" and has been taken over by artificial intelligence. A milder version of this theory is simply that we're overrun with bots. Most of us take that for granted at this point.

But I think the sheer volume and scale of what's coming will be meaningfully different. And I think we're unprepared. Or at least, I am.

2/2 Passing the Reverse Turing Test

Our new challenge as little snowflake humans will be to prove we aren't language models. It's the reverse turing test.

After the forest expands, we will become deeply sceptical of one another's *realness*. Every time you find a new favourite blog or Twitter account or Tiktok personality online, you'll have to ask: Is this really a whole human with a rich and complex life like mine? Is there a *being* on the other end of this web interface I can form a relationship with?

Before you continue, pause and consider: How would *you* prove you're not a language model generating predictive text? What special human tricks can you do that a language model can't?

We're about to drown in a sea of pedestrian takes

The Dark Forest Theory of the Internet

An explosion of noise that will drown out any signal

A. Triangulate objective reality

As language models become increasingly capable and impressive, we should remember they are, at their core, linguistic prediction systems. They cannot (yet) reason like a human.

They do not have beliefs based on evidence, claims, and principles. They cannot consult external sources and run experiments against objective reality. They cannot go outside and touch grass.

In short, they do not have access to the same shared reality we do. They do not have embodied experiences, and cannot sense the world as we can sense it; they don't have vision, sound, taste, or touch. They cannot feel emotion or tightly hold a coherent set of values. They are not part of cultures, communities, or histories.

They are a language model in a box. If a historical event, fact, person, or concept wasn't part of their training data, they can't tell you about it. They don't know about events that happened after a certain cutoff date.

I found Murray Shanahan's paper on Talking About Large Language Models (2022) full of helpful reflections on this point:

> "Humans are members of a community of language-users inhabiting a shared world, and this primal fact makes them essentially different to large language models. We can consult the world to settle our disagreements and update our beliefs.
> We can, so to speak, "triangulate" on objective reality."

Talking About Large Language Models, Murray Shanahan

This leaves us with some low-hanging fruit for humanness. We can tell richly detailed stories grounded in our specific contexts and cultures: place names, sensual descriptions, local knowledge, and, well the *je ne sais quoi* of being alive.

Language models can decently mimic this style of writing but most don't without extensive prompt engineering. They stick to generics. They hedge. They leave out details. They have trouble maintaining a coherent sense of self over thousands of words.

Hipsterism and recency bias will help us here. Referencing obscure concepts, friends who are real but not famous, niche interests, and recent events all make you plausibly more human.

B. Be original, critical, and sophisticated

Easier said than done, but one of the best ways to prove you're not a predictive language model is to demonstrate critical and sophisticated thinking.

Language models spit out text that sounds like a B+ college essay. Coherent, seemingly comprehensive, but never truly insightful or original (at least for now).

In a repulsively evocative metaphor, they engage in "human centipede epistemology." Language models regurgitate text from across the web, which some humans read and recycle into "original creations," which then become fodder to train other language models, and around and around we go recycling generic ideas and arguments and tropes and ways of thinking.

Hard exiting out of this cycle requires coming up with unquestionably original thoughts and theories. It means seeing and synthesising patterns across a broad range of sources: books, blogs, cultural narratives served up by media outlets, conversations, podcasts, lived experiences, and market trends. We can observe and analyse a much fuller range of inputs than bots and generative models can.

It will raise the stakes for everyone. As both consumers of content and creators of it, we'll have to foster a greater sense of critical thinking and scepticism.

This all sounds a bit rough, but there's a lot of hope in this vision. In a world of automated intelligence, our goalposts for intelligence will shift. We'll raise our quality bar for what we expect from humans. When a machine can pump out a great literature review or summary of existing work, there's no value in a person doing it.

C. Be original, critical, and sophisticated

The linguist Ferdinand de Saussure argued there are two kinds of language:

1. La langue is the formal concept of language.
   These are words we print in the dictionary, distribute via educational institutions, and reprimand one another for getting it wrong.

2. La parole is the speech of everyday life.
   These are the informal, diverse, and creative speech acts we perform in conversations, social gatherings, and text to the group WhatsApp. This is where language evolves.

We have designed a system that automates a standardised way of writing. We have codified *la langue* at a specific point in time.
    What we have left to play with is *la parole*. No language model will be able to keep up with the pace of weird internet lingo and memes. I expect we'll lean into this. Using neologisms, jargon, euphemistic emoji, unusual phrases, ingroup dialects, and memes-of-the-moment will help signal your humanity.
    Not unlike teenagers using language to subvert their elders, or oppressed communities developing dialects that allow them to safely communicate amongst themselves.

D. Consider institutional verification

This solution feels the least interesting. We're already hearing rumblings of how "verification" by centralised institutions or companies might help us distinguish between meat brains and metal brains.

The idea is something like this: you show up in person to register your online accounts or domains. You then get some kind of special badge or mark online legitimising you as a Real Human. It may or may not be on the blockchain somehow.

Google might look something like this:

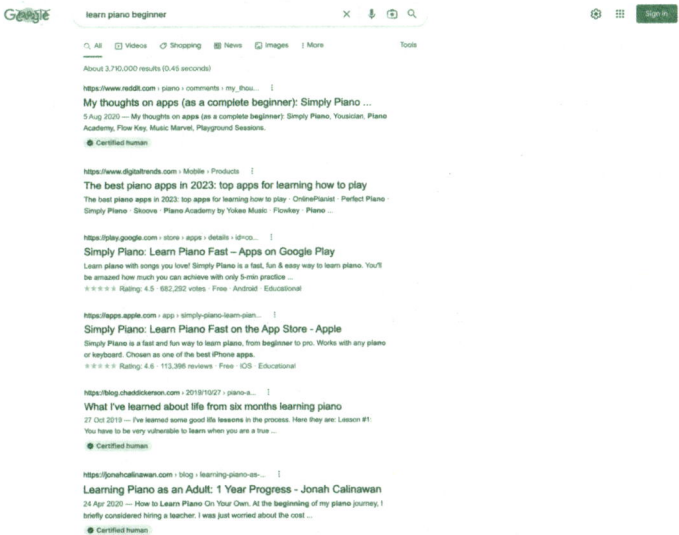

The whole thing seems fraught with problems, susceptible to abuse, and ultimately impractical. Would it even be the web if everyone knew you were really a dog?

E. Be original, critical, and sophisticated

The final edge we have over language models is that we can

prove we're real humans by showing up IRL with our real human bodies. We can arrange to meet Twitter mutuals offline over coffee. We can organise meetups and events and conferences and unconferences and hangouts and pub nights.

In Markets for Lemons and the Great Logging Off, Lars Doucet proposed several knock-on effects from this offline-first future. We might see increased fetishisation of anti-screen culture, as well as real estate price increases in densely populated areas.

For the moment we can still check humanness over Zoom, but live video generation is getting good enough that I don't think that defence will last long.

There are, of course, many people who can't move to an offline-first life; people with physical disabilities. People who live in remote, rural places. People with limited time and caretaking responsibilities for the very young or the very old. They will have a harder time verifying their humanness online. I don't have any grand ideas to help solve this, but I hope we find better solutions than my paltry list.

As the forest grows darker, noisier, and less human, I expect to invest more time in in-person relationships and communities. And while I love meatspace, this still feels like a loss.

31.03.2023

Holographic Media
by Caroline Busta and Lil'Internet

Last summer, we were having dinner with Shumon Basar when he raised a question: What will the next era of media be? As a prompt, he spouted off a shortlist of recent media eras: mainstream, indie, social, recommendation... At the time, "vibe shift" was trending, crypto was crashing, and Russia's war in Ukraine raged without reprieve. Fukuyama's declaration of the "end of history" was once again up for debate.

As we know from media theory à la McLuhan, a shift in the dominant media apparatus alters not just how content circulates, but the kind of content we make, and the types of responses people have to it. When we talk about "generations," we are speaking about age cohorts differentiated by media eras and how they shaped a sense of reality. TV's signal galvanized young Boomers around the cultural revolutions of the 1960s. The rise of desktop publishing, consumer-grade music samplers, and home video recorders gave Gen X the hardware for a media environment both democratized and comparatively decentralized. By the '00s, an internet networked according to IRL friends and self-selected interest groups radicalized Millennials away from top-down media. But horizontal, user-directed social media would soon be disrupted by a protocol capable of algorithmically tailoring information to each user's individual digital activity. Recommendation media typifies the information sphere of Zoomers.

Importantly, each era of technology has a unique "physics"—a term we use to describe the hard-coded mechanics and incentives of every media platform, whether digital or analog. Users are as bound to these conditions when operating within a given platform as they are to gravity when walking on Earth. Platform physics are the ways in which a medium's design determines a piece of content's nature, the content's "natural motion" through a network, its recipients' responses, and the various nth order effects of this content being in circulation.

Consider the physics of the monthly art magazine. The format was correlated to the rhythm of gallery shows (also monthly), allowing time for consensus around an artist's new work to percolate through a scene before the critic's word influenced the reception. Twitter, by contrast, is built around features such as the retweet that incentivize rapid virality, creating a power law for content where a small first-mover subset attracts outsize attention before more nuanced takes can be formed. The differing physics of these two platforms produce two different kinds of criticism, and arguably, two different kinds of audiences.

A major shift in media protocol in the 2010s compelled the two of us to leave our professional positions in publishing and the music industry. We had spent our twenties learning the rules of one game, but a new one took hold circa 2012, and the existing infrastructure couldn't absorb the shockwaves. Audiences fragmented. Music labels went broke due to streaming. Longstanding print publications had to go digital-first, often making their content free. In turn, record deals dried up, writers' fees plummeted, and across the board compensation for culture-sector work was offered in the form of (rapidly devaluing) "exposure." Critical terrain turned into a virtual swamp of signs and information starved for context, where only the most sensational content wins.

As the media space grew noisier, paths around the mess of algorithmic social media emerged organically in the mid-2010s.

As we and others have theorized, this emergent zone external to web2 platforms might be thought of as a "dark forest" or "cozy web" region of media, a semi-anonymous yet paradoxically more personal space of communication: the group exchanges on Discord, Telegram, WhatsApp, Signal, etc.) not indexed by search engines on the clearnet—the publicly accessible internet — and therefore not governed by clearnet physics. (For more on this, see Yancey Strickler's "The Dark Forest Theory of the Internet," Maggie Appleton's "The Dark Forest and the Cozy Web," Venkatesh Rao's "The Extended Internet Universe," Peter Limberg's "Clearnet, Dark Forest, Darknet" and Caroline Busta on contemporary counterculture.)

Those spending time in dark forest spaces often continue to use Web 2.0 platforms. But while most of us probably still check the main feeds daily to get a current pulse, they are no longer our primary sites of communication. Nor are they the sites of identity formation that they once were. Feeds have become something like interstate roadways with posts as billboards—fleeting pieces of information that momentarily make us laugh or annoyed, and that occasionally compel us to exit.

Present-day media should be taxonomized not by format or scale or genre but by how well they compose their own media ecosystem — how nimbly an outlet can work across various platforms and protocols, from clearnet to dark forest. Noting the importance of this skill, political scientist Kevin Munger said: "If you and your community do not have a concrete set of norms, practices and institutions designed to allow you to use the internet without the internet using you—you are destined to lose. In fact, you're not even trying to win." The more varied an outlet's spread of plat-

forms, the less beholden it is to any single one.
The less bound it is by any one platform's physics.

Essentially, the capacity for composability emerges as an indispensable quality of our current mediascape. Composability is already a popular concept in crypto circles, where it refers to building "protocols" rather than platforms, and portability of a community across platforms through token-based social graphs. But we see it extending beyond web3 systems. Already in the mid-2010s, dark forest groups had devised ways of finding each other across constellations of platforms (whether by including key emojis in one's bio — a pine tree, a frog, a black fist, a rainbow flag — or through sharing content from certain meme pages so members of an enclave can synch their clearnet feeds). Structurally, what these communities were doing was composing their own media networks. They were forging a social protocol where the community signal is stronger than the pull of any individual platform. We might even say that the community itself becomes a form of media, a holographic filter through which every platform is accessed and where individuals with strong connections across multiple communities become literal inter-faces for information.

To understand what this new era of community as media looks like, imagine the Web 1.0 webforum—multiple nodes arranged in a circle, each equally connected to the others. Now imagine the Web 2.0 attention-driven network: a sea of individual influencers connected unidirectionally to tiers of followers. In a composable community-as-media model, a protocol synthesizes both. Members of a shared network interact in a non-gamified, horizontal way — as in webforums — while also broadcasting across social media feeds, cross-pollinating their community's thoughts and attracting new members.

With this new media schematic in mind, let's now speculate on some of the phenomena this media era may produce.

⅙ Voiding the Mid

In *The Extreme Self* (2021), Shumon Basar, Douglas Coupland, and Hans Ulrich Obrist spoke of the "100ocracy"—the power of the middle of the bell curve—making the point that online, scale always wins and therefore the average is king. But this principle doesn't only apply to entertainment, retail products, and narrative production; it equally applies to exploits and scams. This is why a Windows computer or Android phone is far more likely to get a virus. There are simply more Windows and Android users and so bad actors have more opportunities for success by targeting these operating systems rather than others. The optimal place to be is on the left or the right of the curve.

As cybercrime explodes and AI-enabled bots multiply the already dominant average, we anticipate a voiding of the Mid, especially on social media. Younger generations are already suffering from Mid-exhaustion as endless culture-warring and grandstanding didacticism have made "using your voice" on social media seem extremely cringe. And if you think the spam and scams are already bad, just wait. The first AI to achieve sentience could very well be a Men's Rights Activist who earned a fortune emptying the bank accounts of high-net-worth individuals by emulating their voices.

2/6 Avoiding the Mid

Illegibility. Poetry. Speaking even more in diagrams, images, metaphors, collages, neologisms — forms of language that AI (and the Mids) do not yet understand. These are tools for avoiding the Mid-void. Another strategy? Bringing back the sanctitude of True Names. When something's or someone's True Name is known, it can be exploited for attention and other economies. Giving a True Name allows for indexing, search engine optimization, and for that thing or person to be consumed by the Mid. Dark forest spaces allow True Names to be better protected, or kept hidden entirely.

3/6 Dark Forest Expansion

Beyond the voided Mid, dark forests will proliferate. In the digital and in the real, we need to plant more trees. Everyone will belong to one or more of these dark forest communities, and will need to defend their culture from spammers and scammers from the Mid.

4/6 Scam Realism

Scamming on a societal scale has been a constant in the world for those who have grown up in the twenty-first century. The late-'90s dot-com bubble? The result of a now-classic scam where internet companies receive a ridiculously high valuation because, theoretically, the total addressable market is every single person who can access the internet. That bubble quickly popped but it's a great scam and we love it. We still do it today! In the early '00s, George W. Bush gaslit the West into believing the Iraqis did 9/11. Then the Obama administration convinced 70 percent of Americans that the Islamic State was "the number one threat to American interests." Defense contracting go brrrr. The financial crisis of 2007–08 rounded out the decade, and its reverberations continue to destabilize the global economy. Crypto is a scam, too, and everyone knows it. OK, blockchain is not inherently a scam, but the scam potential in recent years was just too big to not scam. Uniquely, crypto created a massive, social media-based scam, with hundreds of thousands of people actively evangelizing ideas they believed only because there was a monetary incentive to do so. Crypto's True Name, however, was spelled out in the rubble of the FTX collapse, and now, hopefully, its scamming has passed its peak. In America, virtually every ad on TV is for pharmaceuticals or sports betting. Apps are engineered to be maximally addictive, siphoning as much time and money as they can from "users." Young people are fully immersed in an addiction economy—it's all one big scam, and they know it. Scam Realism is the paradigm of the now, because scamming is the water in which we all swim, even if we twentieth-century dinosaurs try to not admit it.

5/6 Influencers Sensemakers

When there's so much noise and so much scamming, where do we find truth and who can we trust? Overwhelmed by the sheer volume of conflicting information, hot takes, scoldcore, and didactic thinkpieces from the Professional Managerial Class, people increasingly trust only those to whom they're directly connected — whether personally, or parasocially. And this is why non-institutional figures — Substack writers, artists, podcasters — and their wider communities will continue to fulfill the role of Trusted Sensemakers. Meanwhile, corporations and governments will need to cultivate relationships with these sensemakers in order to gain broader trust—and traction.

6/6 Think Meta

And so, smart twenty-first-century natives think meta. They think the way our Tech Overlords think. Why build products or services when you can control and therefore capitalize on the infrastructure through which every exchange takes place?

To gain agency in today's media space, you need to overcome the physics of its software. By thinking meta, you can build new protocols, structures that allow truth and trust to emerge. Whether through blockchain tools, new nested internets, or meta-assemblages of various platforms and apps, the future of media will come from experiments taking place at the level of protocol. And through these new protocols, new complexities will emerge through new relationships — complexities that we should embrace. Worldbuilding together, we can keep True Names secret, protected from the homogenizing force of the Mid, allowing for a return of productive incoherence, uncertainty, deep wisdom, and magic.

-

Text adapted from a talk for Global Art Forum Dubai, 2023

Dark forests will proliferate. In the digital

The Dark Forest Theory of the Internet

and in the real, we need to plant more trees

Caroline Busta & Lil Internet · CH.3 Holographic Media

Editors do not make magazin

2000

EVENT / STIMULUS  ⟶ **LEG**

CRITIC/JOURNALIST
CREATES PRIMARY SIGNAL

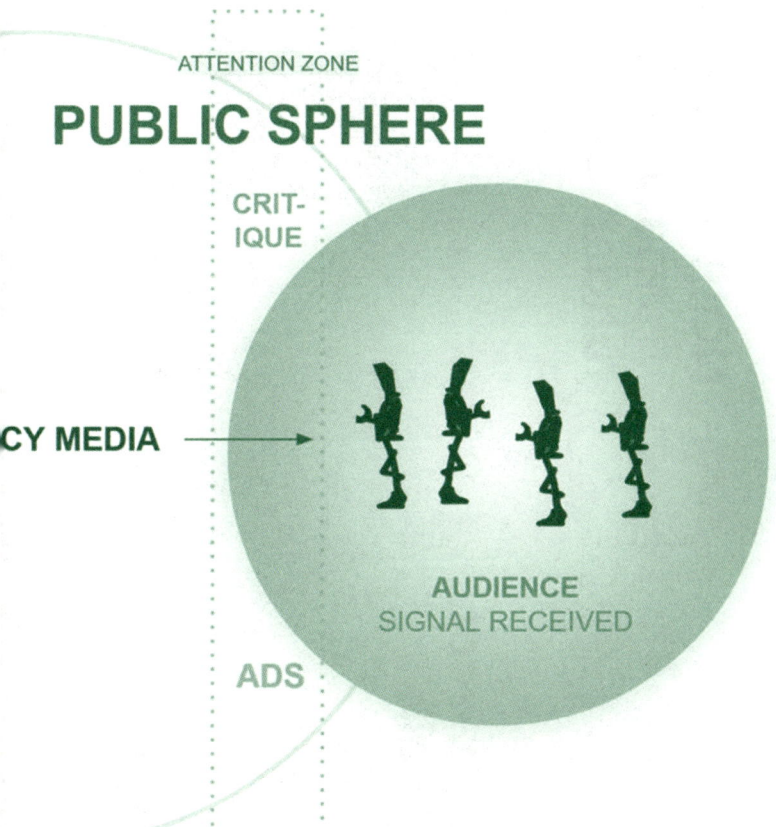

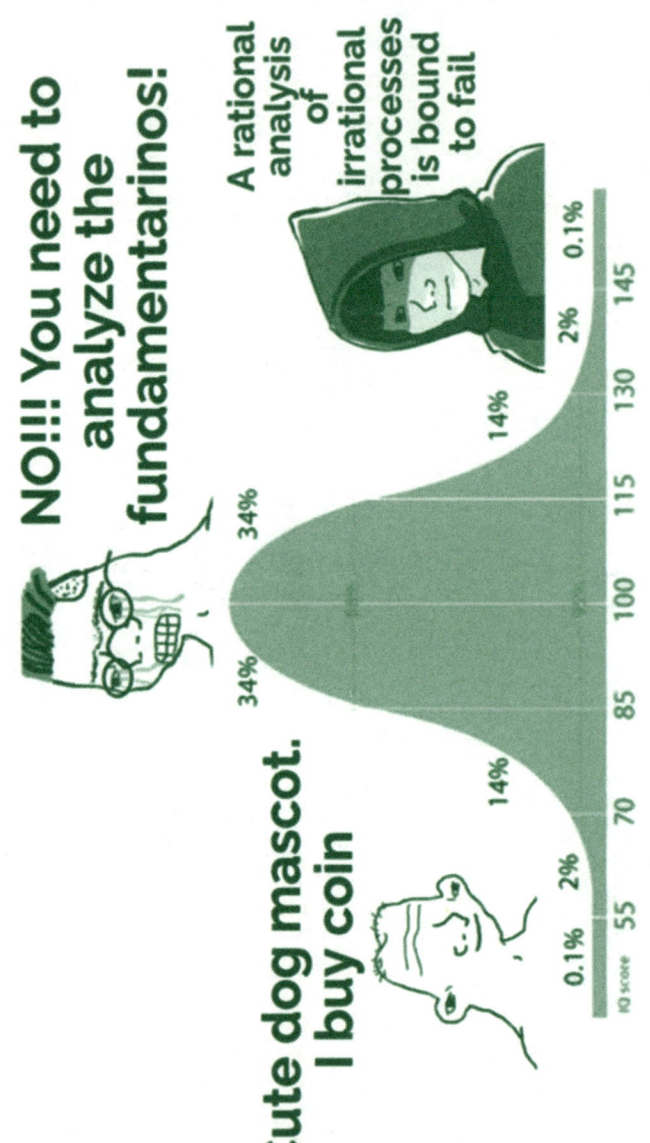

THE VOIDING OF THE MID

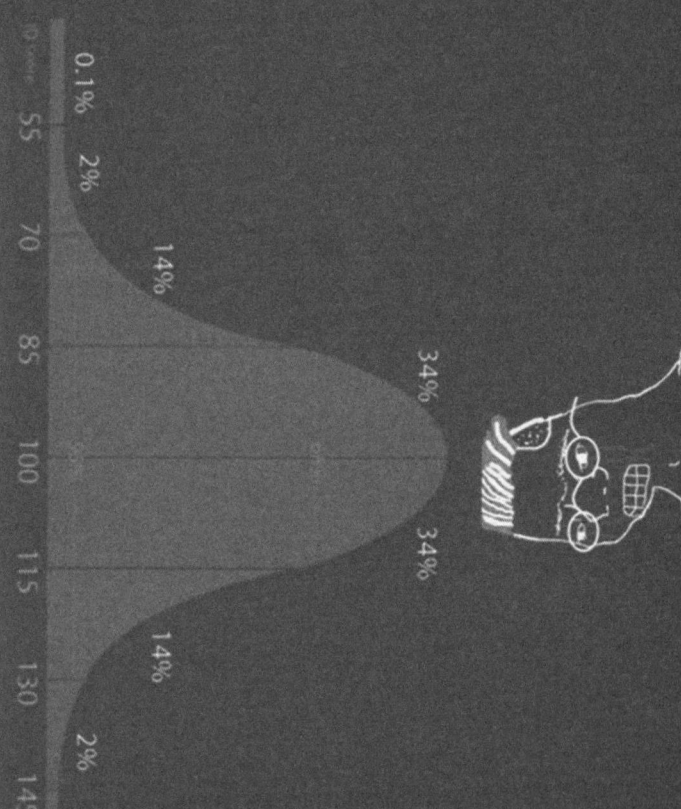

VINGE

ames
Cyberspace Frontier

Kellen

Angel

Serena Saint Germain

B2B
crisislarper   Ferran Steve

REMILIA

MILADY MAKE
RAVE THREE

- DOT COM BUBBLE
- 2008 FINANCIAL CRISIS
- ADDICTION ECONOMY
- SCAM

PHILADELPHIA

IRAQ WAR

CRYPTO BUBBLE

...NATED AND
...TO COMMIT
...K FRAUD

...REALISM

HOLOGRAPHIC VIBES
INDEPENDENT COLLECTIVE
PERSONA

TRUST

SUBSCRIPTIONS	SUBSCRIPTIONS	CLOUT
PUBLIC GIGS	COMMRCL GIGS	TOKEN VALUE
BOOK DEALS, ETC	PARTNERSHIPS	

THINK ~~∞ Meta~~ META

NETWORK A

NETWORK B

NETWORK C

01.09.2023

The post-individual
by Yancey Strickler

On the internet we can be whoever we want to be. We can choose from any number of qualities, real or imagined, and express ourselves and live our lives from that point of view online.

To go online is to become re-individualized — an individual in a whole new way and place. You still exist in the physical world, but you gain a new social existence that floats over-top of, around, inside of, and as a force within almost all other areas of life.

Because of the internet we don't need to define our identity based on where we physically live, who we're born to, or what we look like, as has been the case in human history until now.

The ability for people to separate themselves from their geographic, familial, and physical realities by creating new identities continues to reshape the world more than we realize. Computers and the internet have changed how we see and understand who we are, how we socialize, and inspired humans to act in ways closer to how algorithms and machines see us: segmenting the micro-personas and qualities within us into distinct alts and platform-specific identities that can take on lives of their own. We're in the midst of a significant evolution in what it means to be an individual.

This experience and confluence of forces is what I call post-individualism — a term intended to capture the ways computers and the web have changed our sense of self and how society is changing in response. While these dynamics are new, they echo the experiences of our ancestors that led to the creation of modern society as we know it, and even earlier societies too.

¾ Kissing Cousins And The Origins Of Individualism

Our story starts more than a thousand years ago around 1000 A.D. when humans were going through a series of changes not dissimilar to what we're experiencing now.

As recounted in two excellent books, *The WEIRDest People in the World* by Joseph Henrich and *Inventing the Individual* by Larry Siedentop, roughly 1,000 years ago was when the modern concept of the "individual" — someone with agency in what happens in their life socially, professionally, romantically, spiritually — gained momentum in Western society.

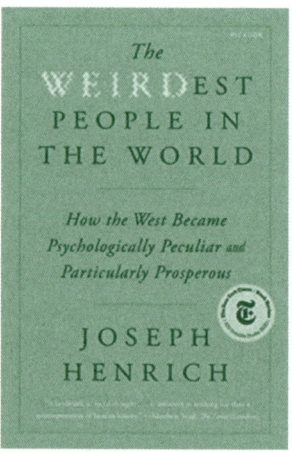
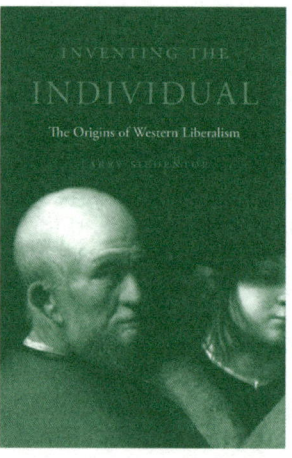

Before this turning point, civilization was less a teeming throng of diverse masses than a collection of closed miniverses bound by blood. The vast majority of people lived among extended families in clan-like settlements. As Henrich writes in *WEIRDest People in the World*, the family was the first religion. Who you were born to defined your whole existence.

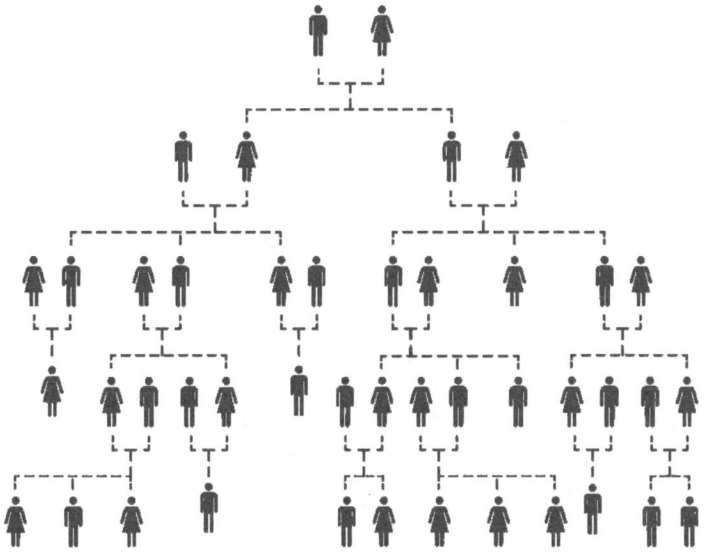

One way families would preserve power was to marry cousins to each other. Yes — cousins. Cousin marriage reinvested the family's power directly into the future fortunes of the clan.

For centuries, cousin marriage was a dominant force. But about a thousand years ago, its prominence began to decline because of a surprising source: Christianity.

In the ancient world where wealthy and influential men held virtually all power and all others were seen as lesser beings, Christianity's promise of universal salvation was a liberating secret that gave each person the right to their own inner purpose. As Christianity spread over the next thousand years, spiritual equality and, along with it, individualism did too.

Around 1000 A.D., Christian churches pushed individualism from the spiritual to the physical. Leaders of the Catholic Church, potentially intending to break the clan-based power that dominated their parishes in Southern Europe, issued a decree: it was forbidden for first cousins to marry. Within decades, the custom of intra-cousin marriage began to decline. The structure of society changed along with it.

For non-cousins to marry, places and ways for people to arrange marriages and find a partner were needed. New spaces and customs arose. Within a century of the Catholic Church's prohibition, three major institutions of Western history became newly prominent: the city, the guild, and the university. All either had their growth take off (cities) or were largely invented (the guild and the university) within roughly a century of cousin marriage's prohibition. Some of the deepest foundations of modern society started because families weren't allowed to marry first cousins anymore.

⅕ Individualism

What happened to those first individuals?

Neither Henrich or Siedentop's books cite personal experiences documented by people living at the time, but seen through the lens of broader social changes that began in this era, we can make some educated guesses.

The rewards of individualism weren't the right to be left alone, they were the right to choose who to align yourself with. The first individuals used their freedom to seek other people with whom they could live, work, love, raise families, and study. They (men, in particular) gained more sovereignty over their lives.

This need for alignment was critical because left on their own, early individuals were vulnerable. They risked being robbed, harmed, and exploited by others. They lacked easy entry to a trade. They were limited in what they could be or do.

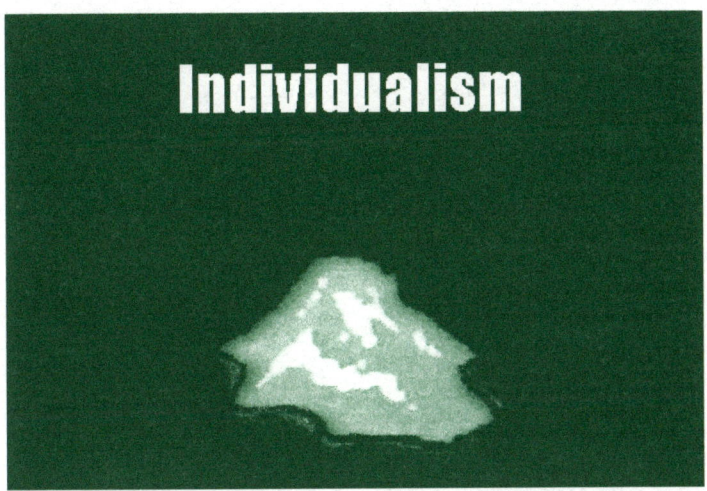

As this process of people seeking safety and opportunity repeated generation after generation, trading posts grew into villages, villages became cities, and repeated interactions became institutions. The first university opened, attracted students, and gained influence. More followed. Guilds that provided a regimented path to work in the trades were established in increasing numbers of professions. As these institutions grew, more and more people left the countrysides for these bustling assemblies of individuals. Within centuries power shifted from the blood of clans to organizations of individuals, and the individual-driven system overtook the clan-based system it emerged from.

This process is why today disputes are settled by independent courts rather than family elders. It's why I introduce myself as Yancey Strickler or just Yancey rather than Son of the Stricklers or however my ancestors said things. This isn't true everywhere, but in many parts of the world today the family is less the focus than the individual because of these changes.

By the end of the 20th century this process played out to such an extent that people were expected to stand out on their own as individuals. To self-actualize as "Me" became the pinnacle of social success. The human experience became reoriented around an individual's need to self-actualize through consumerism, as recounted in Adam Curtis' documentary series *The Century of the Self*.

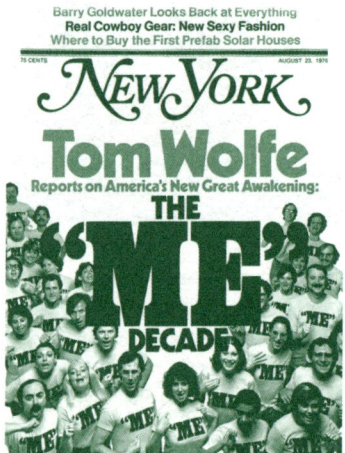

The force of individualism created a world of abundance for many. But in the most individualistic societies (the U.S., U.K., and Australia top the list) the costs included growing loneliness and the decline of social institutions.

A 2021 study reported: "The role of friends in American social life is experiencing a pronounced decline... Americans report having fewer close friendships than they once did, talking to their friends less often, and relying less on their friends for personal support." We had reached this line of individualism's final form: isolated, shrink-wrapped humans ready to self-actualize with each purchase.

2/5 Post-individualism and the Self

This changed, like almost everything else, with the internet.

The internet opened up a new inner-outer virtual world where our thoughts were typed, confessed, searched, expressed, and manifested with the thoughts of others. A world where we became born again as individuals in a new realm.

No longer were we constrained by physicality or geography. We could be whoever we wanted to be. We could be however many we wanted to be. Our inner lives multiplied. This change came not just with the internet, but with the emergence of its underlying medium: the computer.

In 1984, M.I.T. professor Sherry Turkle published *The Second Self*, a sociological survey of the first computer users, including schoolchildren, secretaries, and stockbrokers in the 1970s and early '80s. Turkle observes from the very beginning that a computer wasn't like a normal tool. Deborah, a middle school-age girl, tells her:

> "When you program a computer, there is a little piece of your mind and now it's a little piece of the computer's mind... and now you can see it. I mean, the computer can be just like you if you program it to be, your thoughts, your pictures, your feelings, your ideas, not everything, but a lot of things. And you can see the things you think and change them around."

Turkle observes:

> "Technology catalyzes changes not only in what we do but in how we think. It changes people's awareness of themselves, of one another, of their relationship with the world. The new machine that stands behind the flashing digital signal, unlike the clock, the telescope, or the train, is a machine that 'thinks.' It challenges our notions not only of time and distance, but of mind... The question is not what will the computer be like in the future, but instead, what will we be like? What kind of people are we becoming?"

As the title of her book observes, computers and especially the internet change how people feel about themselves. They open up new notions of self and new forms of identity. In part because we learn to see ourselves the same way computers do.

Ben Thompson, author of the technology publication Stratechery, once illustrated in an essay how the internet had shaped his identity with a simple visual:

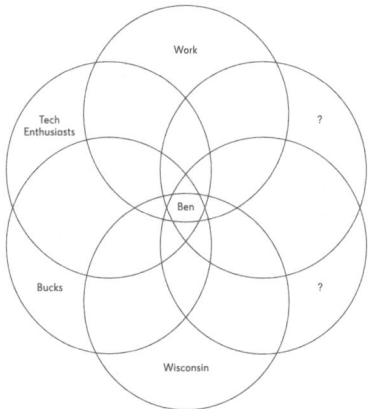

As an individual, Ben (the circle in the center) is the amalgamation of many distinct interests and identities. Each of the petals of the Ben-flower represent a part of his life and who he is. Because of the influence of social media, Ben sees these dimensions as identities to make distinct and further invest in. He writes:

> "Separating my identities on Twitter does not mean a lesser experience, but a far superior one; social interaction in any medium is always a balance between self-expression and the accommodation of others, which means that in the analog world it is a constant struggle to strike a balance between being myself and annoying everyone around me at some point or another.
> The magic of the Internet, though, is that you can be whatever you want to be."

Earlier generations were bound by family, geographic location, and their physical being. People today face few limits on their ability to explore, express, and manifest distinct identities. But our approaches are shaped by the platforms and algorithms we identiate through.

The spaces previous generations filled with close human relationships we fill with identities. This is how people are more connected than ever while being lonelier and having fewer close relationships than any generation in modern memory. We're more connected to the many selves within us than we are to each other.

For individuals before the internet, the key existential question was "Who am I?" After the internet, it's "Who *all* am I?"

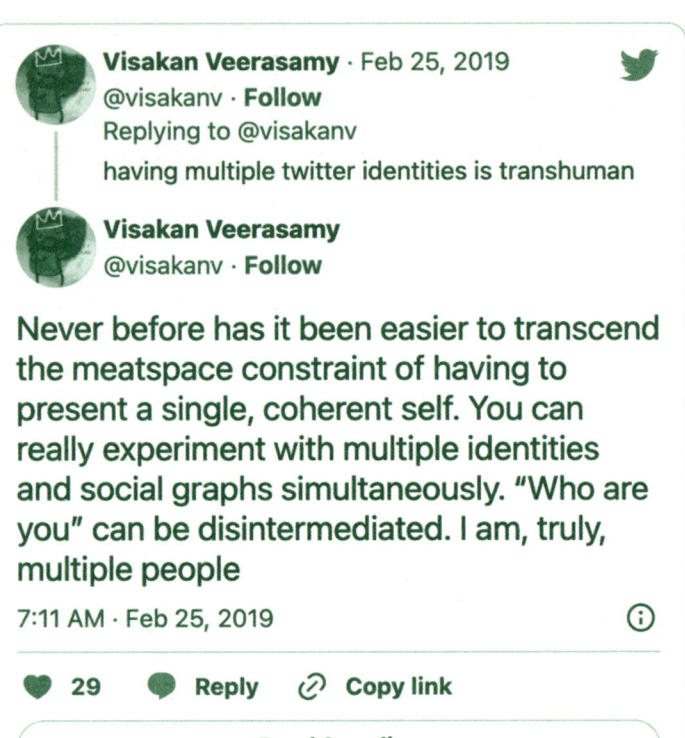

⅗ The Post Individual

Classic individualism is a life-defining question to establish who you are and to grow into that person over the rest of your life. But in a world where the quest for individualism can be started and repeated merely by logging on or creating a new account in a digital world, the meaning of this process has changed. As K-Hole put it in 2014's "Youth Mode":

> "Once upon a time people were born into communities and had to find their individuality. Today people are born individuals and have to find their communities."

This is the post-individual experience. It happens when someone accepts their individuality, but feels called for a variety of reasons (social, creative, metaphysical, financial) to seek greater meaning and context with others. Post-individualism isn't a rejection of individualism. It's a graduation from it.

People are not born post-individuals. Our social environments spark this desire for a specific kind of shared meaning. This especially happens online, where individuality creates the feeling of intellectual and emotional sovereignty, but also makes us lonely, thirsty for attention, and prone to being red-pilled by ideologies that aren't true to our spirit or may harm us and others.

Like our ancestors 1,000 years ago, we're learning that leaving the safety of one's real-world clan can be an isolating and dangerous experience. As I wrote in "The dark forest theory of the internet" in 2019, the web has become the place where powerful forces fight for influence and control:

> "The internet of today is a battleground. The idealism of the '90s web is gone... The public and semi-public spaces we created to develop our identities, cultivate communities, and gain in knowledge were overtaken by forces using them to gain power of various kinds (market, political, social, and so on). This is the atmosphere of the mainstream web today: a relentless competition for power. As this competition has grown in size and ferocity, an increasing number of the population has scurried into their dark forests to avoid the fray."

A thousand-plus years ago our ancestors's need for safety and context sparked the rise of cities, guilds, and universities.

To go online is to become re-individualized, an individual in a whole new

way and place. We became born again as individuals in a new realm

Our current needs as internet-liberated individuals are sparking a similar burst of organizational experiments, including the maturation of Reddit boards, Discord channels, WhatsApp and Telegram groups, and newer and repurposed forms of online communities. These are all post-individual proto-institutions that speak to the desire for safety, meaning, and social, creative, and financial prosperity we as online and offline individuals share.

Tellingly, these institutions are focused less on our entire selves than on aspects of who we are. Like content feed algorithms, the internet grants us the ability to segment our micro-personas into distinct identities that create and join communities with the micro-personas of others. On the internet our inner selves come alive to manifest parallel realities so powerful they're overtaking the world that created them.

Evidence of the post-individual state is abundant:

- A new "whole self": People are used to interacting with each other as surface-level individuals, but today we don't always know how the physical person in front of us matches the multitudes within them. We know not to judge a book by its cover, but now we might not be able to entirely judge a book by its words either. As people learn to carry an increasing number of alts and slices of self, defining who we are becomes more complicated.

    This larger "whole self" is why it can feel safer to interact online where everyone is in avatar mode than in physical environments where our identities are sometimes less clear. What if we discover the stranger is an ideological enemy we did not immediately perceive? How can we act without revealing the values of all our selves? These are questions of inner and outer safety that generations today newly face.

More Gen. Z consumers say they feel most like themselves 'online' than 'offline'

**Percentage of responses by generation:
Where do you feel most like yourself?**

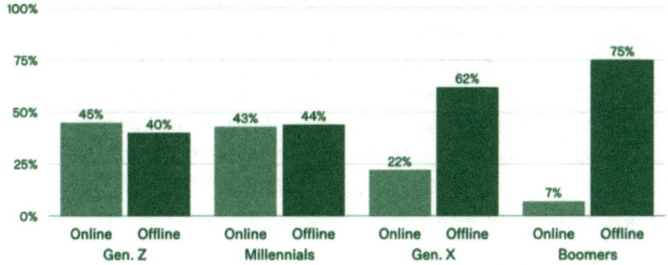

- Post-individual collectives: In an era of individualism, how many followers you have is the key social indicator. In an era of post-individualism, it's what groups you're a part of that matters. The individual isn't erased, it's supported and strengthened by aligning with others. As more of our social and inner lives are lived online, internet-based groups will increasingly be how social value and power are attained. (See the classic "Squad Wealth" by Other Internet.)

  Message boards and internet communities have existed since the start of the internet, but they're becoming increasingly sophisticated. They now have the ability to raise funds, share decision making, and legally incorporate themselves. These internet-first organizations have already proven to be extremely influential online and off, and this will only grow. What the corporation was to the 20th century, online-first collective structures will be to the 21st.

- Identityism: Post-individual dynamics and incentives lead to the proliferation of group identities. The social value of group identities and membership is sparking new categories of identities to emerge at potentially exponential rates. Micro-identities are a path to belonging.

  Many of these identities emerge through minute interests or points of difference between people or groups that can create offshoots and factions. Because our identities are tied to our core values and who we are, differences between or criticisms of ideals or members of our group can feel like criticisms and attacks on us. At times this resembles the clan-driven society that predated individualism with its many miniverses more than what we've known in recent centuries.

- Memes: As in-group collective language and references, memes are a native form of post-individual communication. Learning one's in-group language is a critical rite of passage that proves someone belongs. Memes are core internet communication that have already broken out of the web and embedded themselves deeply in everyday language. These post-individual signifiers reveal what tribes you're a member of and how deep your awareness extends.

4/5 The Century After the Self

In The *Second Self*, Sherry Turkle witnessed immediate changes in human psychology from the invention of the computer. As an interview subject told her:

> "I like to think of my work as 'out there.'
> And I am 'in here.' The thing with the computer is that you start to lose track of the ins and the outs."

I know this feeling first-hand.

	Pre-individualism	Individualism	Post-individualism
Source of power	Clans/bloodlines	Capital + politics	Capital + communities
Social structure	Families	Corporations	Internet-native groups
Religious beliefs	Honoring ancestors	Christianity + the self	Selves + the network
Institutions	The family hearth	Governments + corporations	Networked organizations
Key challenge	Agency + survival	Living wage + alienation	Loneliness + mental health
Strengths	Simplicity + safety	Agency + wealth	Freedom + optionality
Weaknesses	Power concentration	Zero sum competition	In-groups/out-groups
Primary value	Familial power	Individual wealth	Squad wealth
Key metric	Land owned	Wealth accrued	Connections with others

For decades my identity has been in many ways internet-first. My professional development has been almost entirely on the web. I've been a longstanding member of several message boards. I have friendships with people all over the world that began and are sustained online that relate to different facets of who I am that the internet helped me discover. The internet is my social home.

I've experienced wonderful connections and discoveries from this. I've also experienced being on the fringe of so many worlds I don't feel really part of anything. Moments when I've longed dangerously for attention. A lingering feeling of never really belonging anywhere except in front of a screen.

What I've come to realize is that while our potential identities are infinite, our energy is not. Energy put into one identity is energy taken from another. To be Very Online is to be Never Offline. To become infinite is to become infinitesimal somewhere else. As Turkle wrote in The Second Self:

> "For adults as well as children, computers...
> offer companionship without the mutuality and
> complexity of a human relationship. They seduce because
> they provide a chance to be in complete control, but they
> can trap people into an infatuation with control,
> with building one's own private world."

This is something I'm still challenged by. But seeing myself as part of a larger tribe — a post-individual generation seeking meaning and clarity in a new world — gives the struggle context that's comfortably bigger than just my experience.

This also isn't everyone's experience. It's most true for Very Online people who have allowed their self-identity and sense of self-worth to be tied up in these spaces. This is much less true for people whose lives are rooted in real-world communities. The state of the post-individual is not a default all experience the same way. It's a condition of environment. But as generations are increasingly born into digitally native social systems as Gen Z and younger are, the influence of the post-individual state will be an increasingly significant and perhaps welcome part of their lives.

As the journalist Adam Curtis told me in a conversation for The Creative Independent:

> "There are different definitions of freedom. The contemporary idea of freedom is very much an individualist one. I, as an individual, want to be free to do what I want to do... The idea of individual self-expression—whilst feeling limitless because the ideology of our age is individualism—looked at from another perspective is limiting because all you have is your own desires.
>
> [...]
>
> The hyperindividualism of our age is not going to be going back into the bottle. You've got to square the circle. You've got to let people still feel they're independent individuals, yet they are giving themselves up to something that is awesome, greater, and more powerful that carries them into the future beyond their own existence. That's what people are yearning for."

⁵⁄₅ The society of the Selves

In *Cinderella* and *Mrs. Doubtfire*, identity conflicts are resolved by protagonists bringing their diverging personalities together. To marry Prince Charming, Cinderella must admit that it is she, a poor girl and not a princess, who the slipper fits. When Robin Williams comes clean as the boisterous matriarchal nanny, his children love him more.

According to Hollywood folk tales, merging your main and your alt is the moral thing to do. Is that the end game of the post-individual? To merge all our identities into one?

The activist and technologist Pia Mancini once told me about the emergence of a new word in Barcelona: *yosotros* — a combination of "I" ("yo") and "We" ("nosotros") that represents the collective I, the singular We. The term emerged through political movements, but its implications feel bigger. Could this represent a form of collective self? A new pronoun?

In 2021 the artist Katherine Ball told The Creative Independent:

> "I use the pronoun 'they' in my bio… because I like this idea of recognizing that there are more microorganisms living in our bodies than there are of us. The body is an ecosystem. I think somehow, there's another self, more 'us' than 'I'."

In a post-individual society of the selves, this could be a global subculture for how people come to define their identity.

When we bring in the developments of AI, even more significant changes to individuality appear. With most AI models being powerful amalgamations of incredible amounts of human-generated data, the notion of an individual mind could become a relic of the past. It's striking to return to that comment from the middle school girl in the early '80s from *The Second Self*:

> "When you program a computer, there is a little piece of your mind and now it's a little piece of the computer's mind... and now you can see it. I mean, the computer can be just like you if you program it to be, your thoughts, your pictures, your feelings, your ideas, not everything, but a lot of things. And you can see the things you think and change them around."

These changes can feel alarming. But if we go even further back in history, they could be bringing us closer to earlier roots. David Graeber and David Wengrow's recent book *The Dawn of Everything* recounts how early Mesopotamian, American, and African societies moved between individualistic and collective periods based on how people procured food (hunting, individualistic; planting, collectivist) with a fluid complexity to identity and function:

> "The freedom to abandon one's community, knowing one will be welcomed in faraway lands; the freedom to shift back and forth between social structures, depending on the time of year; the freedom to disobey authorities without consequence — all appear to have been simply assumed among our distant ancestors, even if most people find them barely conceivable today."

A frequent shift between individualistic and collective social systems is rooted in the human experience. But the dominance of modern institutions created top-down, hierarchical structures we've forgotten are meant to change.

And now they are.

At this very second, message boards, group texts, social media, dark forests of the internet, and other digital worlds are challenging institutions coded a thousand years ago. The 21st century and perhaps many future centuries will be heavily influenced by post-individualistic, internet-based principles about what a self really is. Online communities have already evolved from one person one vote to one identity one vote. How distant the Victorian Age feels to us now will be what life before the internet feels like for generations to come.

The internet's infinite private worlds at times feel more like the clan-based societies that predated individualism. But where past worlds were bound by blood, today's are bound by interests, desires, identities, and what the algorithms governing these spaces — helmed by capitalistic KPIs —nudge us to do. If the experiences of past generations are a guide, what lies ahead isn't the collapse of civilization. It's the invention of a new one based on a very different idea of what it means to be an individual.

an <u>individual</u> is compr

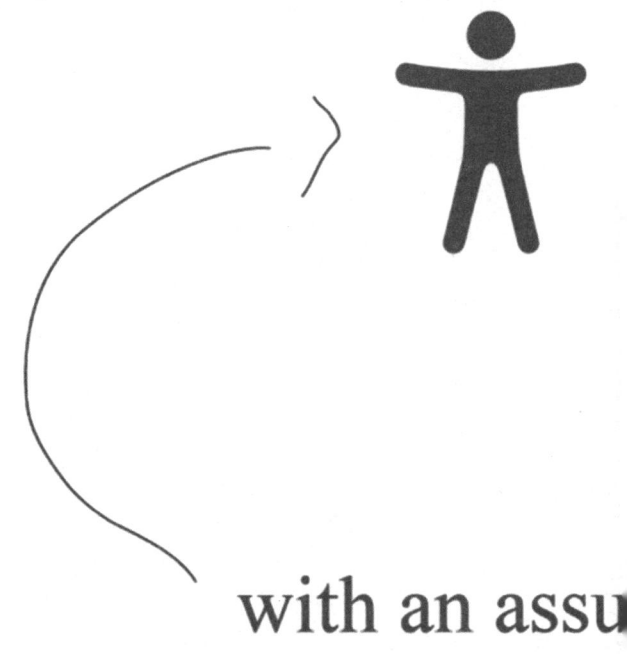

with an assu

ised of multiple selves

ned identity

Illustration by Laurel Schwulst

The Dark Forest Theory of the Internet

Final Words

"The universe is a dark forest. Every civilization is an armed hunter stalking through the trees like a ghost, gently pushing aside branches that block the path and trying to tread without sound. Even breathing is done with care. The hunter has to be careful, because everywhere in the forest are stealthy hunters like him. If he finds other life — another hunter, an angel or a demon, a delicate infant or tottering old man, a fairy or a demigod — there's only one thing he can do: open fire and eliminate them. In this forest, hell is other people. An eternal threat that any life that exposes its own existence will be swiftly wiped out. This is the picture of cosmic civilization."

Liu Cixin, The Dark Forest

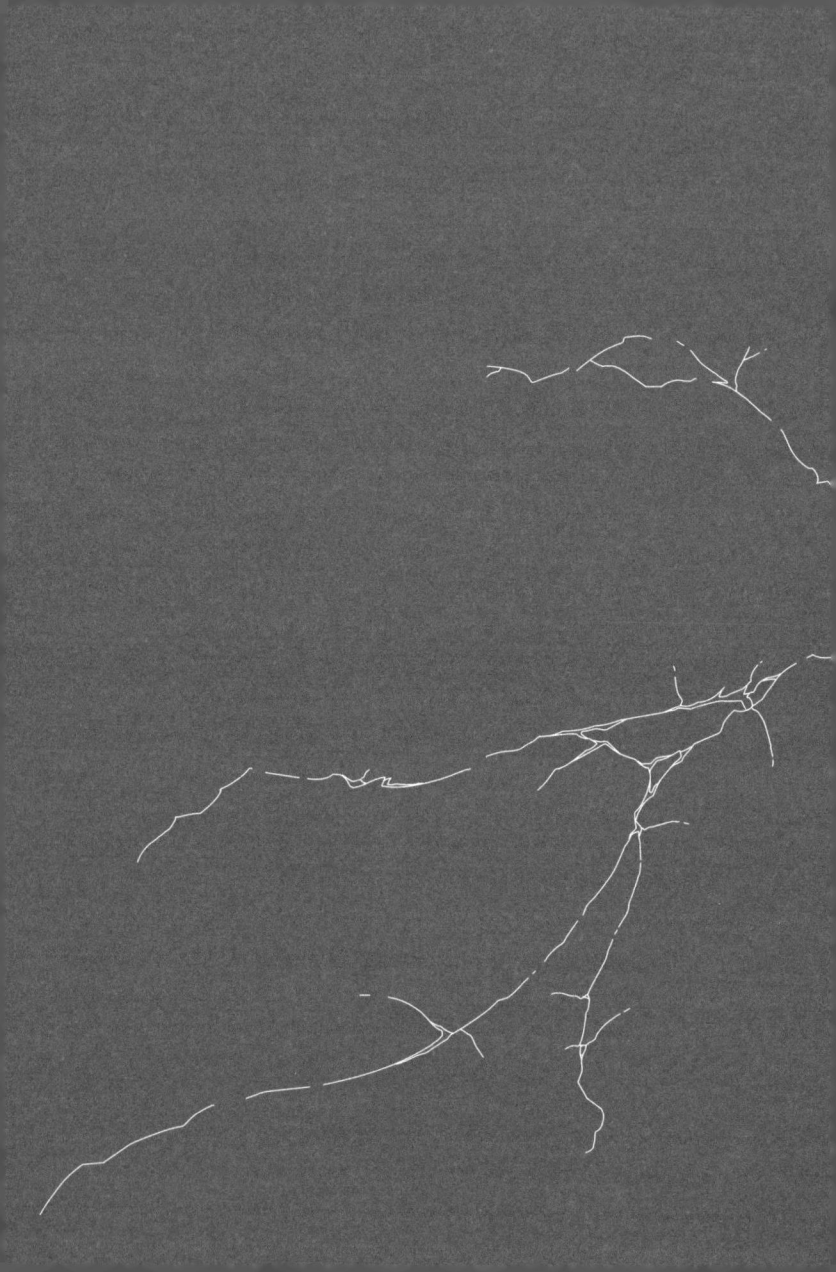

GLOSSARY OF TERMS

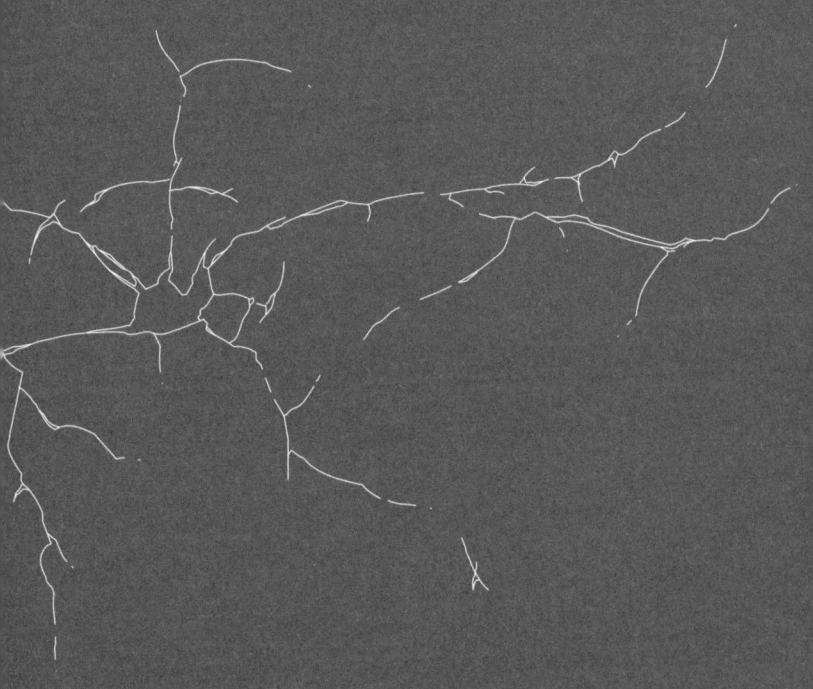

Clear Net

All publicly indexed sites (i.e., big social media, commercial platforms, and anything crawled by major search engines).

Cozy Web

The (human) protocol of everybody cutting-and-pasting bits of text, images, URLs, and screenshots across live streams. Much of this content is poorly addressable, poorly searchable, and very vulnerable to bitrot. It lives in a high-gatekeeping slum-like space comprising Slacks, messaging apps, private groups, storage services like Dropbox, and, of course, email. The cozynet is not the same as waldenponding, since it remains connected and online and isn't concerned about distraction or overuse of digital media. It just retreats from public view/activity for various reasons ranging from simple preference for privacy and small communities to fear and PTSD.

Creator Stadiums

A vast array of podcasts, private newsletters, and video-essays built to highlight individual sensibilities and passions. Creator Stadiums give expression to the thoughts and knowledge of the content creators that use them to communicate with potential and already existing audiences. This sharing of media formats between dark forest communities and Clearnet Stadiums can be traced to their shared emergence on a certain generation of mid-2010s tech platforms such as Patreon, Discord, Substack, and their reliance on the crowdfunding mechanisms that lie at the core of these platforms.

Dark Forests

Online gathering spaces that are non-indexed, non-optimized, non-gamified, and hidden from public view. Typically hosted in Discords, Telegram, and WhatsApp Groups, and other private channels where conversations feel private and contextually safe. Compared to the free market communication style of the mass channels — with their high risks, high rewards, and limited moderation — dark forest spaces are more Scandinavian in their values and the social and emotional security they provide.
They cap the downsides of looking bad and the upsides of our best jokes by virtue of a limited audience.

Dark Net

A digital zone flooded with security concerns, hostile intentions, and lots of associated technology like VPNs and stronger-than-passwords security models. Here the corporate deep web morphs into the government-corporate deep-state web of security and law-enforcement agencies, whitehat/blackhat hackers, and then the dark web proper of cloak-and-dagger conspiracies, drugs, assassination contracts, and worse.

Miniverses

Compared to the generalized idea of the metaverse in which one persistent and shared virtual reality allows for much less customization on a community level, a miniverse is flexible, adaptable, and agile smaller world with its own theme, lores, rules, and potential mechanisms.

Moving Castles

Modular and portable multiplayer mini-verses inhabitedby communities that use them to manage their lore, ecosystems, and economies.

Platform Physics

Ways in which a medium's design determines a piece of content's nature, the content's "natural motion" through a network, its recipients' responses, and the various nth order effects of this content being in circulation. Users are as bound to these conditions when operating within a given platform as they are to gravity when walking on Earth.

Post-individualism

The period when new structures and associations emerge to create safety, culture, shared prosperity, and collective meaning among previously disconnected people. Today's post-individualism is rooted in the internet's ability to isolate each of our micro-personas into distinct identities that can create and join communities with the micro-personas of others.

Proof of Vibes

Vibes are, according to Other Internet, "the ineffable energy that the squad values most" and "an unstable substance of high information density." Proof of Vibes protects a network's security by rendering legible who belongs and who doesn't through language, references, and memes. Vibes always be shifting, and for those who do not stay plugged in, virtual community lore moves much faster than one can keep track of, constantly shifting insider and outsider status.

"Do not answer.

The Dark Forest Theory of the Internet

Do not answer."

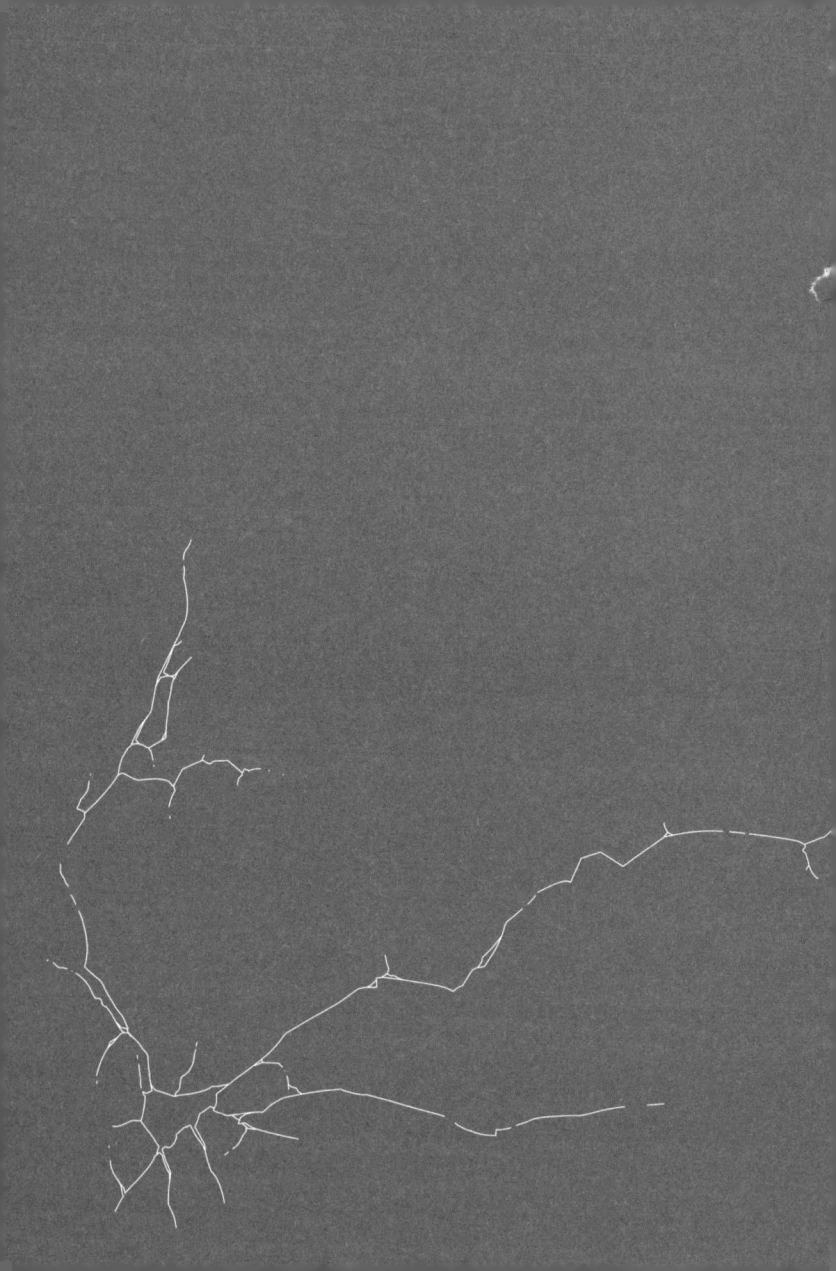

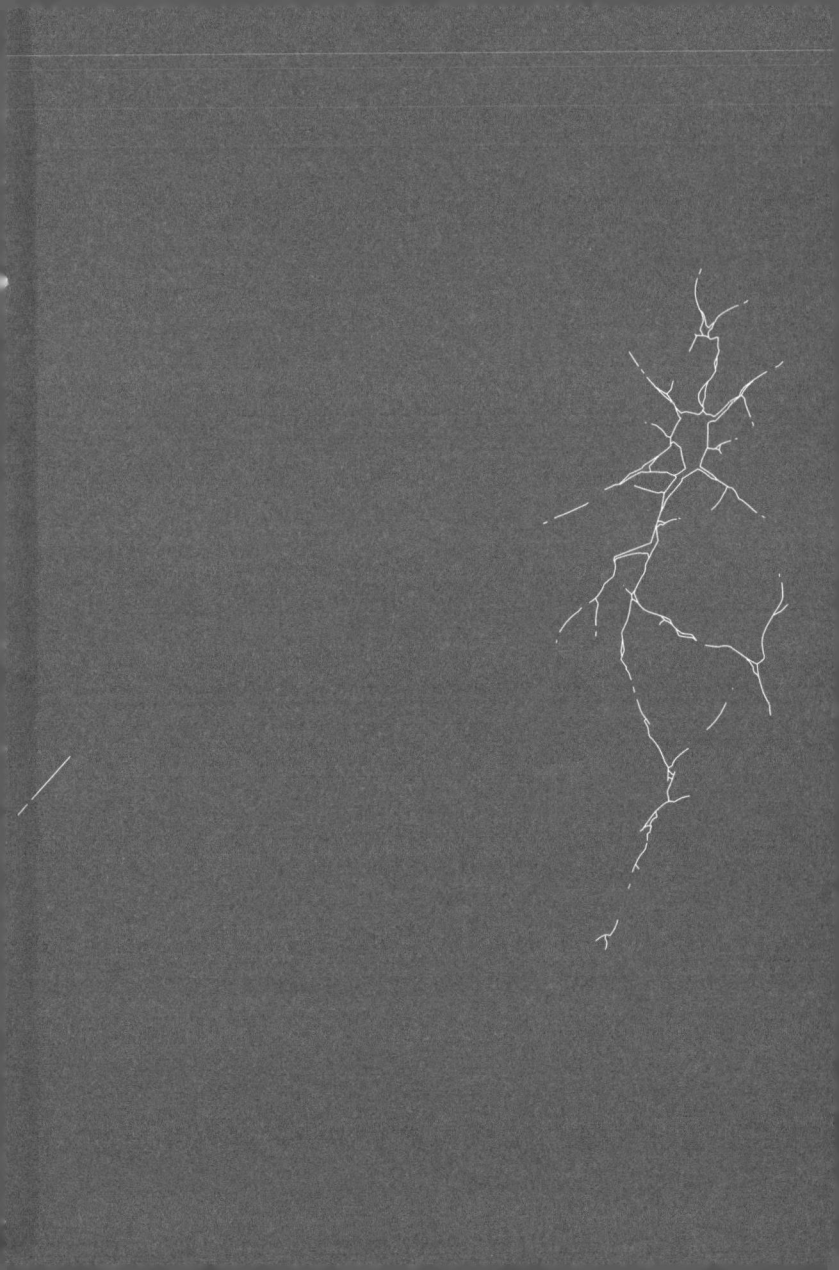

The Dark Forest
Anthology of the Internet

Editor:	Yancey Strickler
Publisher:	Dark Forest Collective
Art Direction:	Leïth Benkhedda
Illustrations:	Stelios Illchuk
Authors:	Yancey Strickler, Venkatesh Rao, Maggie Appleton, Peter Limberg, Rebecca Fox, Joshua Citarella Leïth Benkhedda, Arthur Röing Baer, GVN908, Caroline Busta, Lilinternet
Additional contributors:	Nathan Schneider Laurel Schwultz Ilja Yudanov
Printer:	Druckhaus Sportflieger, Berlin
Fonts:	Neue Haas Grotesk by Christian Schwartz Tonka by Celine Hurka
ISBN:	979-8-218-31123-0
Publication Year:	2024